the EXTRAORDINARY
Family Travel Guide
BUCKET LIST USA

CREATE EPIC MEMORIES WITH THESE
UNIQUE VACATION EXPERIENCES
FOUND IN THE UNITED STATES

JACKLENE CONNER

© Copyright 2022 - All rights reserved.

The content contained within this book may not be reproduced, duplicated, or transmitted without direct written permission from the author or the publisher.

Under no circumstances will any blame or legal responsibility be held against the publisher, or author, for any damages, reparation, or monetary loss due to the information contained within this book, either directly or indirectly.

Legal Notice:

This book is copyright protected. It is only for personal use. You cannot amend, distribute, sell, use, quote, or paraphrase any part, or the content within this book, without the consent of the author or publisher.

Disclaimer Notice:

Please note the information contained within this document is for educational and entertainment purposes only. All effort has been executed to present accurate, up-to-date, reliable, and complete information. No warranties of any kind are declared or implied. Readers acknowledge that the author is not engaged in the rendering of legal, financial, medical, or professional advice. The content within this book has been derived from various sources. Please consult a licensed professional before attempting any techniques outlined in this book.

By reading this document, the reader agrees that under no circumstances is the author responsible for any losses, direct or indirect, that are incurred as a result of the use of the information contained within this document, including, but not limited to, errors, omissions, or inaccuracies.

Table of Contents

Introduction iv
    Family Calls iv

Chapter 1 The Family Vacation 1
    Best Family Vacations 1
    Family Vacation Challenges 7
    The Travel Agent 9
    Takeaways 13

Chapter 2 Family Vacation Tips 14
    Family Tips 14
    Takeaways 27

Chapter 3 Destination #1 Arizona 28
    The Grand Canyon 29
    Takeaways 44

Chapter 4 Destination #2 Las Vegas 45
    The AdventureDome 46
    Treasure Island 53
    SkyPod 58
    Takeaways 64

Chapter 5 Destination #3 Tennessee 66
    Gatlinburg and Pigeon Forge 68
    Takeaways 89

Chapter 6 Destination #4 Wyoming 90
    Yellowstone National Park 91
    Takeaways 112

Chapter 7 Destination #5 Washington D.C. 114
    The National Mall 115
    Takeaways 131

Conclusion 133

References 135

INTRODUCTION

Traveling in the company of those we love is home in motion.
–Leigh Hunt

I remember as a child when my uncle decided to sell up and take his whole family on a trip around the world for one year on their sailboat. At the time, it was quite a risky and rebellious thing to do. Sailing around the world with three kids (all less than ten years old) had many neighbors gossiping. Concerns abound related to their education, safety, uncertainty, and instability, as well as the emotional impact on the five family members on board that small boat on the vast oceans. Let me add that this happened before the technological advancement of smartphones and computers, so we all waited eagerly for news arriving from a telephone call abroad or a postcard from some exotic destination that arrived at Gran's house for the whole family. Of course, we were all jealous but didn't say anything.

He ended up doing this with his family five times. These kids have turned into the most incredible adults. They are well-balanced and content parents with their own families who face the same challenges that all of us have to face, but they have one defining difference—they know how to weather the storms.

Family Calls

Traveling with family can produce some of the most incredible experiences but also some of our worst nightmares! It is crucial to plan the vacation to the last detail to avoid "bad dreams" that can be an overwhelming experience deserving a vacation itself. These days, the enormous pressure on parents from work demands, keeping up at the home front, and also having to plan a magnificent vacation can be exhausting. Yet, we all know the importance of having to recover our health and de-stress. So, I will try to simplify your planning (and all the options!) with some unique experiences that are unforgettable and will create lots of smiles. There is no need to take the same old boring vacation repeatedly. Your kids yearn for more excitement!

Let's find some hidden gems that can be found in the popular vacation spots of the US, like a Boiling River, exotic dinner cruises on the Potomac River, touching the tip of an iceberg, or a heartbeat-shaking thrill ride... which are also perfect for families with kids of various age groups. These hidden gems may make you feel like a kid again as well! The idea is to return from a blissful family vacation feeling rejuvenated, inspired, and happy to be alive. My experience is that we only find that when we travel. When the world overwhelms with all its demands and daily toil, nothing replenishes a weary soul like time away from home. Double that up with adventure and nature, and you have a sure winner.

Like the impressions I learned from my uncle and his unique journeys—effort should never hold us back from an adventure. Life doesn't wait for us; the only certainty in life is continuous change. The growing family is calling...

Chapter 1
THE FAMILY VACATION

Recent studies in 2021 by the Family Travel Association (FTA) and NYU School of Professional Studies indicate that the Covid-19 pandemic affected about 80% of families' travel plans (Turner, 2021). Most of these families had to alter their plans, which didn't appear to be a major concern as long as flexible cancellation policies and clear communications were in place. The study also found that travel advisors are approached more regularly after the Covid-19 pandemic. Health and safety measures are receiving equal priority now when choosing a location. The world is slowly returning to a new normal, and family vacations are happening more frequently.

Let's explore the main points of what a rejuvenating family vacation can do and the importance of the assistance of a travel agent to get the job done effortlessly.

Best Family Vacations

Many parents know the value of taking family vacations to de-stress and rejuvenate "locked-up" emotions. The same survey revealed that post-pandemic statistics indicate a healthy rise in vacation planning. Almost 88% (9 out of 10) of the survey's respondents planned to travel with their families in 2021, after only 44% took vacations in 2020. International travel is also recovering well, and flights are increasing. The vacation trend is indeed stabilizing after lockdown limitations.

Have you forgotten what a family vacation feels like? The benefits of family vacations are priceless. If you find yourself locked in the recovery process after staying at home for so long and having to invent new ways to keep the family occupied and healthy, a trip somewhere else may feel like a little piece of heaven again. Let's look at some options and recover the benefits of spending time together in a different setting.

OVERVIEW

Recent surveys (Turner, 2021) indicate that most families choose to take vacations while visiting family or friends (62%) or taking beach vacations (61%). Close after these two favorite options are visits to theme parks, water parks, and state or national parks. When I think of a family vacation, I think of the blissfulness of not thinking of anything more than the next lunch menu or considering the best complimentary drink for dinner! I think of having the time to watch a sunset uninterrupted while listening to my children's gasps every second before the sun disappears from the horizon as if it plans to never return. I think of their sleepy faces after a day in nature when the sun and breeze kissed their skin while we were all having fun together. Most of all, I think of the laughter—the innocent joy that even lights up the adult faces.

Family vacations are not merely fun but imperative to our mental health and tranquility. Researchers have confirmed that there are significant benefits to taking a break away (as a family) from all the responsibilities of home, work, and school. Vacationing nurtures more healthy family bonding that improves while members are more relaxed. Studies show that shared laughter enhances the feeling of closeness.

The most important part of vacations is the memories. If you aim to create closeness, then the gift of a family vacation will produce far better benefits for the children (and the parents) than a tangible gift. It has been found that they are the best gifts a parent can give their children. They are far more pro-social and connecting than any material gift. You simply have to think of the sensory rewards and emotions arising from vacations like a wilderness safari or the serenity of spa treatment to remember how long they last in the mind. Researchers say that these 'experiential' gifts create profound emotional observations and awareness. Heather Marcoux mentions (2021):

One British survey found almost half of respondents stated that their most favorite childhood memory is one of a family vacation, and more than half (55%) of respondents said 'that these holidays have given them happy memories that will stay with them for the rest of their lives.'

BENEFITS

The 21st century is a changing era, and we are bombarded from all dimensions daily. Technology tends to take over our lives. Social media platforms have become our primary source of social interaction. Smaller families are more favored, and the prevalence of blended families is also higher. A sure way to create positive memories in changing family scenarios is to take a vacation together. Some of the most important benefits are the following.

Unplug
These vacations create a chance to unplug from responsibilities and regular routines. It creates a natural and effortless distance from electronic devices, social media platforms, and smartphones. They create family joy and unplug time while slowing down.

Experience
A family vacation to a different and unfamiliar destination can be a new experience for the entire family. Human beings are naturally drawn to exotic things and adventures because of their curious nature. Why not go and explore these?

Booster
It is also said that memories of family vacations can be like anchors in challenging times. When family members have a few memory resources to reflect on during tough times, they tend to manage difficulties better and stay more open-minded. The positive memories keep perspective levels balanced and assist

with a fresh approach. They boost productivity and positivity back home.

De-stress
They help the family to destress. The combination of quality and quantity time of a vacation enhances the kids' feeling of belonging, family support, and love.

Bonding
They promote family bonding on a big scale, and children and parents see each other in a new light when relaxing together. When removed from the daily grind of life; interruptions by television, computers, and other technology; and other distractions, families are left with living in the moment and interacting with each other. This environment opens windows for families to get to really know each other.

Development
These vacations also help with children's development. Getting out of the usual scenario promotes learning and inquiry. An enriched environment is a natural brain booster for kids. Dr. Margot Sunderland (child psychotherapist and Director of Education and Training; The Centre for Child Mental Health) stresses that new experiences enrich young minds when they combine physical, cognitive, sensory, and social elements of interaction. Even the elementary activity of building sandcastles together produces far better family bonding and brain development in children than wasting time on electronic devices, according to her. Vacation activities also trigger the production of neurochemicals like dopamine and oxytocin in the

brain that leaves a feeling of "all is well" while it is also stress-reducing with bonding elements.

Educational

Family vacations are exciting and educational at the same time. Exploring together cultivates family bonding while it creates shared memories. They open up opportunities to learn more about other cultures and engender open-mindedness with new perspective thinking. When children gather information on-site about new cultures and places, it becomes a visual and interactive engaging education in real-life scenarios. When a child looks into the eyes of an elephant on a safari, they come to understand the animal's soul. They can learn to help them survive extinction. Similarly, when visiting iconic places from the past, like the Colosseum, instead of reading about the life of a Roman in a textbook, children develop a healthy curiosity to know and explore more.

Edu-vacations have become a trendy vacation option for families. They are 'elevated' experiences of learning—blissful experiences outside the regular routine that enhance curiosity. The total immersion and relaxing enjoyment beyond mere culinary discoveries or panoramic wonder enhance new interest, not only for the children but also for the parents. Reconnection with the natural world opens up fresh topics for discussion and awareness. These educational vacations generally aim to encourage appreciation and curiosity for the earth. Children can learn about their history, culture, medicine, traditions, and community in places like Hawaii or a Peruvian Quechua village. When visiting the coral reefs at a resort in the

Maldives, they become more aware of sustainability. The edu-vacations often involve creativity and crafts or environmental awareness as part of the program. If you want an intelligent kid, take vacations to many different locations!

Family Vacation Challenges

Challenges that arise during the planning stage of a family vacation mostly revolve around location and itinerary. Parents find it challenging to keep the whole family happy with their diverse demands and needs. They find it challenging to decide on activity sources that will satisfy children of different age groups and also keep the parents entertained and relaxed.

Studies show that almost half of Americans would like to redo a past vacation because it wasn't perfect in some ways. Mastercard research indicates that about 50% of families plan to take a holiday, but almost 90% of those respondents find the planning time and effort that goes into the trip stressful. Most of these are women. An Omnibus Survey that Mastercard commissioned also revealed that most stress arises from "Getting to, from and through a departing and arriving airport (57%); deciding on a location (50%); developing an itinerary of fun and unique experiences (49%); finding family-friendly accommodations (44%)" (Mastercard, n.d.).

Additional factors contributing to stress are related to payments' safety and security. Most research respondents prefer using a credit card for safety reasons, tracking purchases, convenience, and currency exchange avoidance. The biggest challenges of planning a vacation are the time and effort it takes to schedule and select the accommodation. Another significant issue is finding accommodations for larger families with odd numbers, blended families, or multigenerational family requirements. Many respondents find the overwhelming online or social media information regarding accommodation and location options an additional challenge and would instead opt for a travel agent to assist them.

While balancing savings, family safety, and creating meaningful experiences seem to be a major issue, school break timing also affects choices. It becomes a challenge to customize the needs of children from different age groups and various educational centers, while simultaneously being limited by allotted work vacation time. Additional logistical transportation dilemmas like car travel, flying traveling fears and complications, and additional baggage fees contribute to more stress. Some further issues are the costs of dining out and maintaining healthy sleeping patterns and routines for younger kids.

Then parents also worry about finding rejuvenating adult time while traveling with children. After 2020, the unpredictability of Covid-19 travel influences many choices. Parents are concerned about keeping children safe and healthy while traveling. So, even before the packing challenges, the family may be completely exhausted from all the planning before leaving home. This is why making the process simpler by using a travel agent brings much relief in the planning stages of a family vacation.

The Travel Agent

Planning a family vacation can get overwhelming for the entire family. Therefore, it is much easier to use a travel agent who takes out much of the effort and eliminates the guesswork about logistics, location, and planning. Surveys after the recent Covid-19 pandemic indicate that travel agents are used more than before, and 65% of respondents said that they would use a travel agent in the next two years. According to the US Family Survey of 2019, "16% of parent respondents have used a travel agent to plan and book a trip in the past three years" (Minnaert, 2019), and 53% mentioned using a travel agent again in the future when planning a vacation.

OVERVIEW

Travel agents are qualified advisers who stay on top of travel information. They provide services, including travel packages, that can benefit the whole family while making the most of a logistical booking on behalf of the individual client. They can help a family who plans to take a vacation by assisting and simplifying the complicated and time-consuming planning process. They are also able to help during the vacation with logistics if things unexpectedly change.

Travel agents make everything easier and ensure an enjoyable vacation with the client's particular needs (like financial limitations, school break differences, etc.) in mind. They take away the effort of logistical and informational planning and help the family by supplying research about weather conditions, travel advisories, and current news affairs to comply with families' safety requirements and assist with necessary documents for the trip. They can make a dream vacation become a reality while they help the family.

THE BENEFITS OF USING A TRAVEL AGENT FOR FAMILY VACATIONS

Be Your Advocate

Especially with international traveling, the risks are more significant when not using a travel agent. The costs may be higher and unforeseen expenses may crop up in the long run. Travel agents can resolve unexpected issues that arise before your vacation, at your destination, and after the trip. They can also anchor the best deals while you enjoy the luxury of traveling.

Navigate Complicated Tasks

After Covid-19, travel has become more complicated with unexpected risks and changes. Travel agents navigate around them with first-hand updated information about any new implementations. They have up-to-date information about current happenings and an added extensive and trusted network that gains them additional warning from information suppliers. Changing times requires keeping up to date with the latest info about vaccine travel passports, Covid testing requirements, new resorts, updated airline fare structures, schedules, and so much more.

Save Time, Reduce Stress
Because they keep up to date about national disasters, political upheavals, and unforeseen changes at specific destinations—they can keep you informed with alternatives or advice. They focus on the complexities and thus reduce your stress. You do not want to mess up the next trip. You dreamed about it for many months and saved up over the year to relax and enjoy yourself. A travel agent can ensure that this happens by preventing your vacation from getting derailed by emergency events.

Understand What's Exciting and New
They can navigate new requirements effortlessly through shifting travel restrictions and regulations, as well as negotiate individual changes in logistics. They are also specialists in new and exciting travel happenings like edu-vacations or the latest popular spots with local benefits. They are thus able to provide meaningful and one-of-a-kind vacation experiences. Their knowledge of bucket list items on travel packages and exclusive events also gives you the benefit of experiencing more on your vacation.

Help You Focus on the Fun Part
You simply choose the destinations and leave the sorting out of tedious details to the travel agent. With their personal travel experience and vast network of connections, they focus on giving you back the fun part of a vacation. They consider your specific family requirements regarding room sizes, transportation needs, and dining options and resolve any issues that may arise at the destinations about these requirements.

The Personal Touch
They give you a personal touch and offer customized adventurous activities to create everlasting memories. Travel agents will also consider your unique requirements and make suggestions for your personal preferences. A good travel agent becomes a friend you may need while you are on holiday and something unexpectedly goes wrong—they are just a call away. If you run into problems, it's much easier to call your travel agent than to spend days online sorting out logistical issues while you should be spending time with the family. Have an agent ready to keep the communication going!

Value to Your Travel
Travel agents know the right people in the right places, so they can provide value to your budget and planning with destination perks. They have behind-the-scenes access and can produce unexpected and authentic moments that the average person does not have and that social media do not offer.

Destination Experts
They have the knowledge, connections, and access to special deals at unique destinations, e.g., local cuisine or cultural experiences. They constantly update their research about new happenings at popular destinations and source unique destinations for their clients. In the 2019 travel survey, 52% of American parent respondents said their travel agent had an in-depth understanding of their unique vacation requirements. In addition, more than 40% said that travel agents produce better rates and prices for their destinations (Minnaert, 2019).

Give Special Access

Many travel agents network extensively with cruise lines, resorts, and luxury hotels through which they consistently get access to special features and upgrades. This enables them to ensure you get the best rooms and treatment on arrival.

Takeaways

Just like you allocate your life savings planning to a specialist, assigning your travel planning to a specialist who warrants the best experience with the least effort is much easier. Their knowledge, experience, and connections will minimize the strain of your planning and ensure that you have the remaining energy to go and enjoy that long-awaited family holiday.

In the next chapter, we will look at some general family travel tips to guide you *en route* to the first destination.

Chapter 2

FAMILY VACATION TIPS

> *Family time is the best time.*
> *–Carmelo Anthony*

Let's find some helpful tips to keep in your toolkit during the vacation planning—and on the trip—that will make the experience easier and smoother for the whole family.

Family Tips

Traveling with kids is just parenting in a different location. Be assured that one of the kids will find something upsetting and make their discomfort public. Prepare for this! Using a qualified travel agent is definitely worth smoothing out the planning and booking process and reducing some of the obstacles. Before looking at any of the following tips, make it your number one priority to choose your family destination with care; it may make or break the vacation. For me, this is the most essential factor when planning a vacation with my kids. You want to keep the toddler and the teenager happy at your chosen destination while you can focus on parental de-stressing. After this, meticulous preparation and attentive planning will make your family trip a success, even if some speed bumps interrupt the way.

TRAVEL TOOLKIT TIPS

Take It Slow

Don't cram everything into one day when traveling. Arrive early when you are traveling by public transport, or leave on time when driving. There is always extra time needed for the kid who wants to use the bathroom five minutes before the plane leaves. Also, allocate extra time for each day's outings and plan your schedule to do less in a day; this way, the kids don't feel overwhelmed by too many places to see and too many activities. Keep your schedule loose and flexible because you will have to adapt sometimes. Remember, with a family, everything takes longer than when you are traveling on your own—this is not a student backpacking trip! It's also a good idea to schedule some siesta time each day; this can even be a relaxing stroll in nature or some downtime in the park under shady trees. Nobody will enjoy a day crammed full to the brim with no time to relax.

Overpacking Is a Hassle

Pack lightly! You need to pack only essentials because, at the end of a long day, you will not only be carrying a kid but also all the extra luggage. Don't try to take the home routine with you! There are other kids at the destinations that you plan to visit, so there will be things available to buy for them if needed. By keeping to the essentials when you pack, you are taking less, meaning that you will have less to carry and end up having more space for plenty of souvenirs. Make a packing list, and then make that list shorter. Assign a value to every item that you pack and make doubly sure that it is essential before you drag it along.

Book in Advance

More than flights and accommodation can be reserved in advance to reduce complications. Things that can be pre-booked include private/public transportation, sightseeing tours, museum and theme park tickets, private guide bookings, attraction site reservations, festivals, music shows, and so forth. Some good advice is to make a reservation at the place where you intend to stay so that you can go there straight away, check-in, and rest. After a long day of driving or public transport, the kids will be tired, and everyone will value a good night's sleep before the next activity. When you have pre-booked everything, you have less to worry about and will have more smiles on the go. Reservations and planning in advance allow you to bond and relax instead of having the hassles of long queues at ticket lines or issues when you're checking in at your accommodation. You can also order a basic set of groceries delivered to your place (provided you have your own kitchen) so that you don't have to scramble when the kids want to rest their weary feet after a long day's traveling.

Inform the Kids

Give good explanations to your kids about the trip, and don't assume that surprises will make them happier. It's better to keep them informed so that they know what to expect, especially for first-time travelers. Include any information about the transportation and accommodation logistics so that fewer questions will be asked while you are sorting out flights and reservations on-site. It also provides more excitement when the kids have an idea of the things that they will see and experience. Remember that too many new things in one go will cause discomfort and stress you out more, so keep it simple. When children know what to expect from the trip, they are more comfortable and relaxed, and you all will enjoy the journey more. A good suggestion is to make a basic informative list of activities and options that will be available at the destination (or give them an outline of the destinations) and ask them to choose the ones that they prefer. This will give them an understanding of where they will be going and also ensure more security.

Pre-Pack Snacks

Hungry kids can be a nightmare to travel with (as are some adults!), so make sure that you always have some healthy snacks on hand to keep their mouths happy. If flight delays or other problems arise, you have to be prepared to refuel the family while you wait. Some destinations may also introduce new cultures and strange food to the kids, which may upset their stomachs, or they may choose not to eat the food and then feel hungry shortly after. At some destinations, the food supplies may also be limited or not fresh, so it's better to be prepared for the worst-case scenario and still enjoy your trip. I always try to find accommodation with a private kitchen that gives an option of making our own meals if we cannot find alternative eateries or if the kids do not like the meals at the local restaurants. And I always carry a bag of nuts with me!

Invest in Better Gear

Look at specific features of the gear you take with you. Sometimes it makes sense to pay a little more for gear that will lighten your load and not fail you in the middle of nowhere. Nobody wants to struggle with a baby stroller that is too heavy to carry up three flights of stairs or that doesn't fold up easily while using public transport. Sometimes it's better to take a sling for carrying babies or a carrier backpack when the terrain complicates the use of a stroller (gravel roads, cobbled stone streets, etc., can be challenging for wheels). You want to simplify your life and expect the gear not to break in remote areas. Try to do some online family-friendly product searches and read the reviews before you buy! In some places, it makes more sense to rent the equipment than to drag it all along from home. It depends on how often you may use it and how essential the gear is to your comfort. Renting gear from a local supplier also allows you to have it repaired at no extra cost when it breaks. Bear in mind that a sling or backpack may get uncomfortable for both you and the child when it's very hot, so check area-specific climate predictions before you pack. In colder areas, this may be the better option!

Child Discounts are Real

Ask for savings at accommodation facilities, restaurants, and activities like museums, aquariums, botanical garden visits, etc. If you never ask, you never know. Many businesses encourage children's visits and will gladly give discounts or reduced admission fees, but they don't offer them unless you ask! You are most likely to get discounted rates for kids with bus and train transportation, private guides, site attraction entrance fees, guided tours, restaurants (some have kids eat free options), or reciprocal benefits at some museums. Check their websites before you leave and send emails to confirm discounted fees before you arrive.

Nothing is Perfect All the Time

Don't expect things to be perfect all the time. Traveling with kids means things *will* go wrong! See it as a test of your parenting skills! There is always that one kid who wants to go to the bathroom exactly when the bus leaves or the toddler who makes you turn back to go and fetch their forgotten comfort teddy at the previous lodgings. I always think of traveling with kids as an exciting adventure, *with* a few speed bumps that we can laugh about when we reflect on the irreplaceable experiences that we collect as a family. You may even plan for years to take your children to see Yellowstone National Park, and when you arrive, the headlines tell you that there is a huge fire spreading quickly over the park! Or you arrive at the Statue of Liberty only to discover that she is under construction until next Summer… Accept the fact that there is nothing you can do (no matter how well you anticipate every speed bump) to prevent some things from going wrong. This is perfectly alright and inevitable. When you accept this, you will ensure a less stressful journey for the whole family.

Personal Contact Details

Make sure your kids have your contact information in case they get lost. Kids wander off, but it doesn't mean you are a bad parent when they disappear. And when there are many people around or a high counter behind which they can disappear, you are bound to suffer a few panic attacks on the trip. Make sure that they are safe by keeping your contact details (name, phone number, email address, and local address) on them. Put a contact details note in a toddler's shoes or a deep pocket or on a teenager's cell phone (they are never far away from their phones anyway!) Also, make sure that the child knows where your contact information is. Other safety tips are to let them hold hands while you walk or share parent duties (one buys the train tickets while the other keeps their eyes on the kids). In extreme cases, a little GPS device/tracker on their belt will alert you immediately when they wander off and prevent any distress. With older kids, make definite times to regroup again when you go different ways, and make sure that there is no miscommunication about the venue for this meeting. You can also tell them to pin drop on Google maps so that they can find you even if they lose direction. Make sure all their devices are fully charged for this exercise!

Pack All Basic Medicines

The goal is to make sure that if a family member gets sick on the trip, they feel better as soon as possible so that the vacation can continue. Nothing can make you hate a day as much as medical discomfort in a foreign setting. If some family members have allergies, asthma, diabetes, dietary limitations, etc., make sure to pack their medicines to prevent disasters. Trust me, children get sick, or emergencies happen at the most inopportune times— like 10 PM on a Sunday evening in the remotest place on earth! You want to be prepared for this unfortunate scenario. You never know when some foreign pollen may disrupt your child's health! Always pack allergy meds, asthmatic inhalers, diabetic medications, bee sting allergy treatments, and prescription medications. With the latter, you may also need to take doctor's scripts when you travel across borders and take the medication in its original packaging. This will make it easier to replace in another country. Check destination regulations and limitations when traveling with prescribed meds, and have the necessary documents (and printed copies) or special permissions ready. Some countries have strict rules for allowing medication. Check all vaccine requirements before you leave. I never leave home without a basic lightweight emergency kit that includes medicine for headaches, diarrhea, motion sickness (prevention and treatment), plasters and blister treatment, and ointment to relieve insect stings and bites. I keep this readily available in my essentials luggage. Remember, when you are traveling by plane, children's ears need to be equalized. A helpful tip is to keep their jaws moving by chewing gum or sucking on a bottle. Earache is very painful and will surely have your baby/toddler crying non-stop. New destinations also have different water and food that may upset delicate stomachs, so be prepared for this. When traveling by car in remote areas, be sure to have enough water available in case you have a breakdown. It is advisable to have a food allergy or dietary requirements written down (I make cards in both English and the foreign language to hand over to the restaurant staff, some places do not have internet for Google translate), should you ever have to explain a nut allergy or vegetarianism to a waiter who doesn't speak your language. The same applies to psychological or medical specifics.

Electronic Devices

Bring electronic devices to keep them entertained on long rides. This is one time when being a bit more lenient about screen time makes sense. Make sure that electronic devices are fully charged, and download some movies, shows, and books to read even if the internet is not available. It's useful to bring the children's own earphones that they feel comfortable with as well. Airlines do offer earphones, but they are not always as efficient. Sometimes your child may also want to listen to music while you prefer to enjoy the silence of nature—earphones help with this!

Pack Extra Essentials

Bring plenty of essentials like diapers and wipes if you need them. You may need more of these crucial items while you travel than you regularly use at home. Diapers, wet wipes, and specific milk formulas all need to be at least two to three times more than you usually have at home to ensure comfort. Extra Ziplock bags for smelly diapers when you are unable to discard them and an extra set of clothes for the toddler and the parent are important! Nobody wants to walk around inside an airport for hours while waiting for the next flight, smelling of diapers and milk formula! Have a separate essentials bag close at hand with the necessary toiletries and basic items. Always have extra of the most important things.

Ensure That Flight Times Suit the Kids

Be prepared that flight times may interfere with small children's regular routines. Try to find flight schedules that align as close as possible with this. You do not want to arrive at your destination after numerous flights and other public transport logistics, feeling exhausted and completely overwhelmed. Try to make the journey as enjoyable as possible. I always tell my kids that the journey is part of the adventure; it's not about the destination only. If you are taking short trips, it's advisable to take only carry-on luggage on board the flights so you can skip some of the queues. Always check the airline regulations for this, as they may differ. Try to save time and limit queues with online check-in. Some credit cards offer additional privileges when used for purchases. It may include free travel insurance, premium class advantages to skipping queues, or luxury travel arrangements. It's often worth paying that extra bit to make everyone comfortable while waiting in an airport lounge with all its benefits and little free luxuries.

Children Prefer Longer Layovers

You certainly do not want to run from one flight to the next with three grumpy toddlers in tow, so give yourself that extra time when traveling with public transport. The goal is not to travel fast like when you are traveling alone... Make the journey enjoyable when traveling by car by making regular short stops and making them fun and part of the adventure. Be sure to have items available to keep the kids busy while waiting for the next public transport. Journals and cameras are good options to make them more aware of the journey that they experience. Keep the older ones occupied this way, and make little gift bags filled with new toys for the younger ones that you surprise them with when the layover starts. This should keep them occupied for a while. We all love the novelty of a new toy! On extended trips, you can also buy some souvenirs at each destination which will surely keep the family members content and occupied.

Pack Comfortably

Imagine the trip while you pack: Take a stroll to the beach from the hotel room to consider what essentials are needed at each specific place. Make detailed lists and then make those lists shorter to lighten the luggage. Traveling is much easier with lightweight clothes that pack tightly but still do the job against climate extremes. Be prepared for exposure to rainy weather while waiting for a bus or halfway on your hiking trip. Always have a compact foldaway hat available that you can retrieve easily for sun protection. Keep the sunscreen readily available. Pack clothes that you may need while in transit, on top of your luggage, or in an essentials bag. Many airports have shower options available to freshen up, so make use of these to feel ready for the second leg of public transport. Pack lightly because you may have to carry your luggage up flights of stairs—if you can do without a specific pair of shoes that make the load heavier, leave them at home. Packing in threes is a golden rule for lightweight traveling—one in the luggage/room, one in the dirty laundry bag, one on the *derrière*... And never forget to pack that one essential comfort toy or a favorite book to read. A comfort toy may just help a scared toddler to board a huge plane without tears.

Kids Love Public Transport

Kids get excited about trains, buses, trams, subways, monorails, funiculars, ferries, water taxis, tuk-tuks, public bikes, tricycles, segways, bicycles, etc. Every type provides a new adventure while it gives you the time to relax. It's also quicker and cheaper to use public transport most of the time unless your trip is meant to be a driving adventure with numerous stops. Then you should consider making recreational stops along the way. Many of these can be researched before you leave to help with your planning and time allocation for each stop.

Freedom Feels Good

Give older kids reigns on what they want to see and do by giving them a few options with basic explanations of what to find at your destination, and then let them choose some that they would like to visit. It makes them more invested in the trip and excited about the journey. It also makes you feel younger again when you can enjoy a fun setting like an interactive science museum or an exciting music show!

Hotel Hopping Is Exhausting

Children like to settle down in their lodgings for the duration of the vacation. You also do not want to pack up all their scattered things daily while you travel to your next location. Try to find a family-friendly place and stay a while before you move on. It's also advisable to find a place with a kitchen or, at the very least, a refrigerator and a microwave so that every meal does not have to happen elsewhere. Consider picnics for lunch so kids can run their energy off in a park or on the beach while you can take a short nap under the trees or an umbrella.

Be Flexible

Don't fix your vacation. You will surely be disappointed. Flexibility will guarantee more smiles all around. Life is what happens to us while we are busy making other plans, remember? It's all about being prepared for the speed bumps that may interrupt your planning, right? Things may not meet all your expectations once you reach the destination, and this should not destroy the whole family experience. Prepare all the family members for the possible 'surprises' that may interrupt your days. There are always options and solutions for everything; sometimes, it just needs a little innovation (or a call to your excellent travel agent!). There will be some catastrophes and forgotten or lost items, but when you remember to pack your sense of humor and lots of lightweight patience, you should be able to cope well with these little mishaps.

Identification Is Crucial

Make sure that all children have their IDs at all times. Never travel without an identity card or passport for every member of the family. Keep your travel docs handy and updated, make copies, and keep a pen if you have to complete or sign anything. Sometimes you may need documents, like birth certificates, notarized and translated into English as well as a foreign language. Cross-border checks may also require letters stating that you have the right to leave and enter a country with the children, so have these with their IDs available at all times. When traveling as a single parent, some borders may request a permission letter from the non-present parent. Always make sure to inform yourself about destination-specific regulations beforehand, and keep all the original documents (plus more than one copy of each document) in your essentials bag. Some museums require identification before you can enter, and if any accidents happen during the trip, you want some form of ID available immediately. These documents should always be kept safe and easily available. I keep proof of these documents on my phone, and most of the time, they are sufficient.

Takeaways

The whole idea of family travel is to ensure that every member has fun throughout every part of the journey. The most essential part of any adventure is enjoyment! And most of this enjoyment depends on your initial planning and preparation. Now that you are fully prepared for your U.S.A. family vacation let's find some of the most unique destinations to create your epic memories. First, we will go to Arizona!

Chapter 3
DESTINATION #1
ARIZONA

The glories and the beauties of form, color, and sound unite in the Grand Canyon.
—JOHN WESLEY POWELL

Photo by Sonaal Bangera on Unsplash

It is no wonder that the Grand Canyon is one of the seven natural wonders of the world. With its majestically imposing cliff walls that become the palette of the sun, the mighty 279-mile-long Colorado River brushing through, and the sheer vastness of the area that it covers, it keeps everyone in awe of its imposing grace. The Grand Canyon is 277 miles long, with an average width of 10 miles and a mile-deep gorge. There has been much debate about its age, and even today, it remains unknown despite extensive research done to determine the origin of its course in ecological history. The area was first encountered by humans about 12,000 years ago. It's famous for its unpredictable weather extremes, with average monthly high temperatures reaching more than 30 degrees than its lowest temperature ranges. Thunderstorms, windy conditions, high average Summer temperatures, and flash floods are common occurrences. There are many fossils to be found in the park—scorpions, dragonfly wings, and other rock impressions abound—dating back to the earliest geological times. Fossils have been found from the Precambrian time of 1.2 billion years ago! In this chapter, you will learn about one of the world's most ancient wonders in the state of Arizona and discover why it should be at the top of your family vacation list.

The Grand Canyon

The Grand Canyon offers a multitude of experiences for visitors. It receives around six million visitors annually, and there is no reason why you shouldn't be one of them! Be sure to keep your eyes on the park updates page to remain in touch with any temporary closures, alerts, or changes.

OVERVIEW

The Grand Canyon is bordered by the North Rim, the popular South Rim, and the West Rim, where you'll find the famous Havasu Falls. The North and South Rims fall under the management of the National Park Service, the West Rim is managed by the native Indian Havasupai tribe, and the Havasu Falls belong to them. The mighty Colorado River, which runs through the canyon, gets an annual 22,000 visitors on commercial raft trips. The river has 160 sets of rapids, with each their individual rating system on a scale of 1–10, and it requires a high level of technical skill to navigate these rapids. Colorado River rafting remains top of many people's bucket list items.

It is one of the best places on earth to see the gap in rock records between the Cambrian and Precambrian periods, which happened 485–540 million years ago. Scientists call it the Great Unconformity, and it leaves many questions for further research and discovery. It boasts some of the oldest exposed rock formations on the earth, as old as 1,84 billion years, and the canyon started forming as long as 70 million years ago already. Archeologists have found incredible artifacts in the canyon dating back to the Ice Age. Spearheads, split-twig figurines shaped like deer and sheep, and ruins that date back about 12,000 years which accommodated early humans, have all been discovered in the canyon. Six thousand archaeological sites are recorded in the Grand Canyon National Park.

In 1919, the Grand Canyon opened as a national park managed by the National Park Service, but the park only covers some areas of the canyon. There is only one remote town called Supai Village, which falls on the Indian Reservation. Its inhabitants are all people of the Havasupai tribe, and the village can only be reached on foot, by mules, or by an occasional helicopter ride. A visit to Supai and Havasu Falls is a highly sought-after experience.

The Grand Canyon is located in northwest Arizona, bordering Utah and Nevada. The best time to visit the park is during Spring when the temperature ranges are less extreme, and the weather allows for abundant outdoor activities. The North Rim is closed in Winter because of snow. There are many reasons why a visit to the Grand Canyon should be your priority. Apart from the range of iconic activities available to tourists, the area presents some of the most incredible scenery on this planet. It also holds enormous historical and ecological information to be explored—it was declared a World Heritage Site by UNESCO. Because of all these diverse features, it is by far one of the most appropriate destinations for families, and every member will find something epic to discover in the canyon.

THE GRAND CANYON ACTIVITIES

The Rims

Overview

The Rims are the outer peripheries of the canyon and expose the layers of rock, creating walls about a mile high. They reveal the sedimented layers of the earth that formed over billions of years. They are a magnificent sight to see during the different seasons and parts of the day.

The two main Rims are the South and North Rims. The South Rim is more populated and more sought-after, with many tourist attractions and accommodation facilities close to Flagstaff (a 90-minute drive away). The North Rim has only one lodge (The Grand Canyon Lodge) and a campground accommodation facility for visitors. This is the best option for people who prefer fewer crowds and a slightly more isolated adventure. The West Rim is outside the national park, and here you can find the Grand Canyon Skywalk that extends over a section of the canyon. It is not for the fainthearted, as you walk on a horseshoe-shaped glass floor that extends about 70 feet over the scenery. The Skywalk is a bit controversial but a unique experience for young ones. The West Rim is close to Las Vegas.

Activities

The range of activities at the Grand Canyon is endless and will keep any nature enthusiast happy. Whether you thrive on adrenaline, love to camp by a river, want to enjoy relaxing family time with young kids, visit one of the remotest areas in the canyon, have educational fun, cruise the river, watch native American dance performances, swim in azure waters, experience a Wild West train ride *en route*, or simply bask in the wonders of nature with a sunset cooler in hand—the journey to the canyon will provide them all.

Biking the Rims is a popular activity for families as well as fitness enthusiasts. You can rent a bike on-site, and all bicycles are adjusted to fit riders of different age groups. They have user-friendly 7-speed gear mechanisms, and E-bikes are also available. If you would like to camp with your bicycle, backpack camping sites are available at Mather Campground on the South Rim. An array of biking trails meander along the Rims. The most popular one for families is the eight-mile-long Hermit road, which is closed to traffic from mid-March to mid-October, so it is safe for cycling with younger kids. Most of the trails offer enjoyable and relaxed cycling, and the shuttle services have bicycle racks if you prefer to do a one-way cycle and return with the shuttle service. Three interconnected mountain biking trails are available near the South entrance, ranging from a gentle three miles up to a nine-mile circuit. Shorter hour rides or day rides can be done on these trails. There is also the Arizona trail, 24,2 miles long, which starts on the inside of the park and traverses along a section of the rocky Coconino Rim.

The best option to experience the Grand Canyon up close is to book a guided bicycle tour. These can be booked between April and the end of October, and knowledgeable guides take you along the quiet and unspoiled South Rim trails. The trails are not too strenuous, and younger kids will enjoy the engagement with magnificent scenery, spotting wildlife, and getting in touch with nature. Three popular routes ranging from 1.5 hours up to 6-hour rides cater to varied fitness levels and vacation time frame schedules. These biking tours are a good alternative if you do not want to go backpacking down the canyon: You still manage to get out of your car and experience nature face-to-face.

The Grand Canyon is a hikers' paradise with many trails to choose from. A short walk to the Shoshone Point lookout is ideal for young kids and families who prefer a relaxed hiking experience on level ground. For families with adventurous kids, I would suggest the Bright Angel Trail, which covers the 5,000-foot drop down to the Colorado River (where you can camp overnight) but is only nine miles in distance with an overnight midway stop. It does require some fitness, but active kids should be able to do this. The beauty of this hiking experience is that you can switch off from civilization completely, with no cellphone reception available down in the valley. Although the deathly names of some of the trail sites (Phantom Ranch—only reachable with a mule train right at the bottom of the canyon, and Devils' Corkscrew—which zigzags through some of the oldest rock formations in the Grand Canyon on the way to the campsite) may scare you, don't be alarmed. With proper preparation and protection (for heat or slippery parts of the path when it's covered with ice), the family will love the adventure. Make sure you have enough water and quality hiking gear to make it down and up again! Don't attempt this trail with flip-flops!

It's best to start the trail early in the morning to avoid the midday heat. You have to carry everything with you for the overnight stay if you camp, including food and sleeping gear, but the magical experience will soon release you from the weight that you have to bear. There are Havasupai granaries, rock art, and other ruins to discover along the way. Make sure to find out where to look for these before you leave. Hiking among these ruins and traces of the past evokes nostalgia and respect. If you are lucky, you may spot one of the largest North American land birds—a rare California Condor. They were reintroduced to the park during the previous century and have multiplied to about 80 in total in northern Arizona and Utah.

There are two rest-houses along the way to the first overnight camping spot called Indian Garden, which feels like a desert oasis and almost like sacred ground as the memory of past lives lingers in the lush vegetation. The next leg takes you to the river and Bright Angel Campground, where you can enjoy the sandy shores of the Colorado River, complete silence apart from nature's hum, and isolation from the rush of the world. After spending a night or two here under the imposing cliffs and the brightness of untouchable starry skies, you will have more than enough enthusiasm to climb the 5,000 feet back up toward the top.

Another shorter hiking trail for younger kids is the 1,7-mile-long Trail of Time path from the Verkamp's Visitor Center to the Yavapai Geology Museum. On this trail, children get to discover the glory of the ecological time span of the canyon's rock layers. Various exhibitions along the way and walking guides are available at both ends to enliven the exploration. Rock samples can be viewed and touched, and the ecological timeline over millions of years is marked on the path.

A variety of Ranger programs are offered on the South Rim at the park (at Grand Canyon Village and Desert View Village) almost daily during Summer, and they are worth attending. These informative programs are entertaining, free of charge, and offer a range of interesting topics about the park, its history, geology, architecture, some mind-boggling topics, aviation, etc. Some topics that spark interest in the evening programs at McKee amphitheater are *Arthropods through the Ages, Grand Canyon in the Wild Wild West, Ghosts That We Knew, Furry or Ferocious?,* and *From the Canyon to the Moon.* The evening programs last about an hour, and children must be accompanied by an adult. Desert View Sunset Talks also happen frequently at the amphitheater close to the Desert View campground, a short scenic drive away on State Route 64 to the East from Grand Canyon Village. Programs are weather permitting, and all information can be obtained online and from the Visitor Centers.

Apart from these informative and interesting talks, the younger ones can follow a Grand Canyon Junior Ranger program (free of charge) and obtain their own certificate of completion and badge on-site! The children learn about the importance of and how to preserve and protect national parks as Junior rangers. They are encouraged to share their knowledge and maintain the protection of the environment outside the park as well. All they have to do is to collect their age-specific booklet, complete and include their observations and creative components, as well as attend one program led by a ranger. The following badges can be earned:

- Raven award: 4–7 years
- Coyote award: 8–10 years
- Scorpion award: 11 years and older

On presentation of their certificates at the book shop, a sew-on patch can also be purchased to display the honor. The more advanced Phantom Rattler Junior Ranger (from ages 4–14) special patch can be earned on top of this by hiking or mule riding to Phantom Ranch at the bottom of the canyon after completion of the booklet and ranger program.

One of the top things to do in the Grand Canyon is guided river rafting, cruising, or kayaking. For families with kids older than 11 years, I would highly recommend a group or individual-led expedition on the river. The non-profit organization, *Grand Canyon Youth*, offers a safe and educational rafting experience with a focus on natural history, the arts, and science, while still showing respect for the tribal ancestry of the area. Professional guides row the rapids, and children are tasked with leadership, daily chores, and outdoor skills. The expeditions range from one-day up to 17-day trips, and scholarships for funding are available. These epic adventures will be remembered forever and have an enormous impact on their development.

Other river rafting trips offer families a more relaxed journey and frequent stopping along the way to explore ancestral Puebloan sites, experience the spectacular solitude and beauty of nature, spot unique wildlife, or simply swim in azure water. These rafting trips can extend up to 18 days with camping sites alongside the river. They can be done on oar boats or motorized rafts. If river cruising is in your blood, the Colorado River's calling should be the first one to listen to!

One of the most adventurous ways to experience the canyon is through guided tours, of which there are plenty to choose from. You can opt for a jeep tour, a customized helicopter ride, have fun with rafting tours, or a mule ride down to the Colorado

River. Skydiving or zip-lining tours are also available for the more adventurous and older kids. More relaxed options include a bus tour or a train ride to the canyon. Most of these tours will ensure lifetime memories and magnificent scenery.

Park Rangers also offer guided 30-minute tours on weekends to various interesting sites. An incredible archaeological site with a spiritual feel is the sacred area of the ancestral Tusayan Pueblo village, dating back to 1185 C.E. Some of the cultural artifacts and the ruins can be seen at the Tusayan museum, where children can learn more about the tribes and their cultural ways. The people who lived there are believed to be the ancestors of the Hopi and Pueblo communities from Arizona and New Mexico.

An exciting alternative is the annual Star Party, when the whole park changes into an observatory. Grand Canyon is an International Dark Sky Park that offers exceptional stargazing because of its remoteness from city lights and the absence of pollution. You will have unobstructed views of millions of stars, and the vastness of the sky is overwhelming. During the Star Party, free informative astronomy programs and volunteer expertise from telescope viewings are available.

The Bucket List Experience

Havasupai

Havasupai is the tribal Indian name for The People of the Blue-Green Waters. The village of Supai (tucked away in its remote seclusion at the bottom of the canyon alongside Havasu creek) has been the tribe's home for over 1,000 years. The stark contrast of their environment between clear blue-green water and cascading falls, draped against the red earth—scorched and formed by unpredictable weather patterns and relentless heat—makes one stand astonished with respect for their survival in this harsh desert landscape. It's a truly breathtaking natural wonder that must be seen. You can hike between the five Havasupai waterfalls—Navajo Falls, Havasu Falls, Mooney Falls, Fifty Foot Falls, and Beaver Falls—which are all spectacular sights to see.

This opportunity of a lifetime is ideal for active families with older children and teens. Because of its complete isolation, remoteness, and challenging journey to get to the falls, it's not a recommended adventure for younger children. No roads lead to Supai! It's a steep hike of ten miles, and you have to carry all that you need with you—including water, food, cooking-, and sleeping gear. You (and the kids) need some backpacking experience to do this hike. The rough sloping terrain, extreme heat conditions, and shadeless dry terrain make the conditions feel more challenging. Some preparation is required before attempting this wonder of nature. Once you arrive at the falls, though, your life will blissfully change forever.

The booking system is a challenge, and because of the high demand for visits, you have to secure your reservation (including the permit to stay) well in advance. It comes with a bit of luck as well because you have to register on their website and be ready to jump when the bookings open. Normally the campsite and small lodge book up within 30 minutes! No telephonic bookings are allowed. Once you have secured your reservation, meticulous preparation should launch your adventure.

The best location to start your journey to the falls is on Highway 66, about six miles east of Peach Springs. The closest towns to where the trail starts are about two and a quarter hours away at Kingman, Arizona (take Route 66 east, turn left on Indian Road 18, and continue for 60 miles until Hualapai Hilltop Parking) or Williams, Arizona (start on the I-40 west toward Route 66, and then turn right onto Indian Road 18.) From here, at the Hualapai hilltop, you can start your hike. The initial drop is quite steep through the red sandstone until you reach the streambed. Then you walk another seven miles to reach the village of Supai and continue along the oasis of Havasu creek for another two miles to the campground. It's advisable to start this journey early in the morning to avoid the scorching midday heat on your hike to the falls. And remember to carry all your water on the hike down because you can only fill up again once you reach the falls!

Once you arrive, after your jaw-dropping day of hiking, at the tropical paradise in the canyon below, you can either stay at the no-frills Havasupai Lodge or the campground alongside the gurgling creek and the lush vegetation. Prior booking is essential, and the tribe limits the number of visitors to maintain the pristine and secluded experience of Havasu Falls. The lodge has 24 rooms, and the camping area accommodates 300 campers on a non-assigned basis to put up tents. The landscape is fragile, and it's necessary to respect the tribe's strict rules to maintain tranquility. No hiking during the night is allowed, no fires are allowed, and drones, drugs, firearms, or alcohol are strictly prohibited. Hikers are also advised to familiarize themselves with possible flood warnings in the area before they attempt the journey. The facilities are basic—one of the things that makes this place so unique! A little shop supplies a few essentials, and some basic meals can be purchased at a café near the lodge. Besides this, it's only you and nature itself—leaving enough room for unique memories to be built.

Bucket List #1—Havasu Falls

Once you are at the lodgings, you can spend your three or four days doing day hikes to the adjacent falls (and recovering for the steep uphill climb after your visit!) The 100-foot Havasu Falls drop is the most famous of all the waterfalls in the Grand Canyon. Make sure to bring the correct gear for water hopping, strenuous hiking in the heat, and generous amounts of swimming in nature's aqua-blue abundance that hardly ever drops below 70°F. The best time to visit Havasu falls is in Spring and Fall because of the extreme temperatures. The falls are located two miles from Supai village at the campground.

You will never be a complete person unless you experience the breathtaking habitat, abundant wildlife, rock jumping between streams on the creek, and cooling off in the aquamarine holes at the bottom of the falls. Havasu Falls is almost like a piece of magical artwork created to enhance nature. When you observe the crystal clear turquoise water cascading down the red rocks into a blissful five-foot-deep pool in the middle of a desert landscape, your life will pause for a moment, and your heart may just skip a beat.

Bucket List #2 — Helicopter Ride

If the abundance of activities and vastness of the area is too much for you, or if there are time constraints to your canyon visit, another bucket list item is to charter one of the many helicopter ride options over the canyon and see it all from a 45-minute bird's-eye viewpoint. I would suggest a flight that covers the spectacular views from the South Rim to the North Rim. You will be able to see the marble cliffs, the mighty Colorado River, and pines from the national forest all in one go. Doing this helicopter ride at dusk or dawn will enhance the experience, as nature plays along with her color palette. The wraparound views from a helicopter ride give you the most exhilarating experience of the Grand Canyon.

You can depart from Las Vegas or the Grand Canyon airport, and in some cases, the helicopter tours will take you below the Rims for an ultimate and uniquely personal experience of the canyon. From a helicopter ride, you can get a full view of the canyon with all its folds and crevices, exposing billions of years of ecological wonder. It is also a practical alternative to experience the majestic area with younger kids who are not ready for hiking or biking adventures. Whatever helicopter tour option you choose, the experience remains outstanding because you engage with nature from a viewpoint unlike any other.

Bucket List #3 — Rafting Expedition

When I think of the Grand Canyon, I think of river rafting. Apart from the glorious hiking, rafting the rapids of the powerful Colorado River is a top bucket list activity. One of the best options is to take a guided two-day White Water Rafting tour

0009038337

Inspected By: Martha_Aguilar

Sell your books at World of Books!
Go to sell.worldofbooks.com and get an instant price quote. We even pay the shipping - see what your old books are worth today!

with *Victor Tours*, which includes one overnight camping stay and a hike to Travertine Falls. No previous rafting experience is necessary, but visitors have to be moderately fit to take on the rapids with professional guides. The rafts take eight people. This tour includes pickup and round-trip transport from Las Vegas hotels. From there, it's about a three-hour drive (180 miles) to the river and a two-hour drive back the next day. On average, you spend about eight hours on the river every day.

You will experience nine class VII rapids on the river and incredible close-up views of the canyon as you cruise along. The tour takes you paddling through Diamond Creek, Travertine Canyon, and Spencer Canyon. Meals are included, and camping facilities can be rented on the trip to make it easier for you while you only focus on marveling at the landscape and enjoying the thrilling rapids.

Seeing any natural scenery from a river evokes profound emotions. One feels humbled by nature's power, the rhythm of the water determines the time, and a person learns to trust the water to take you to safety. The tranquil moments in between exciting rapids feel like gentle interludes of breathing. The surrounding cliffs of this river, reaching to the sky, make one feel small in the sweeping landscape. Rafting a river in one of the Seven Wonders of the World should not be missed.

Takeaways

- Remember that permits are needed for some of the activities, and most reservations need to be pre-booked well in advance.
- Online pre-booking is essential for Havasupai and rafting expeditions.
- Always pay respect to the sacred ancestral land of the Indian Tribal sites and honor the people.
- Water is life and challenging to maintain in this remote area; always have plenty of water with you.
- Come well prepared, respect the Havasupai rules and Canyon policies, and leave no trace!

We stay with the grandeur of thinking big when we go to see Las Vegas next!

Chapter 4

DESTINATION #2
LAS VEGAS

> *Las Vegas is a city built on hope, dreams, and a little bit of crazy.*
> –MICHAEL MCDONALD

Photo by Grant Cai on Unsplash

While we are still recovering from the magnitude of the Grand Canyon, let's stay with the "everything is bigger" attitude when we visit Nevada. The children will love to experience the glitter and games of Las Vegas—the largest city in Nevada, one of the most famous cities in the United States, and also known as the "Entertainment Capital of the World." I will take you to three of the most popular family-friendly places to revel in the fantasy environment: The AdventureDome, Treasure Island, and SkyPod.

Las Vegas spells lights, amusement, sensation, variety, excitement, glam, adrenaline, and stimulation! The hotels and resorts feel like exotic locations overflowing with luxurious details and extravagance to make you never want to leave. With an arid climate and average temperature ranges between 48 and 93°F, the best time to visit is in Spring and Fall to avoid the extremely hot and dry summers.

Do you want to feel like a kid again? Let's go to a place of magical mystery!

The AdventureDome

The AdventureDome indoor theme park has a wide range of rides and much more to tickle your adrenaline rush and entertainment requests. It also hosts many free entertainment activities and provides guaranteed excitement for young and old.

OVERVIEW

The 5-acre glass-constructed indoor amusement park is the largest in the U.S. and is filled with entertainment and fun. The

AdventureDome offers more than 25 rides and endless activities in a climate-controlled space of 72°F. It's located at the iconic Circus Circus Hotel with its well-known circus entrance on Las Vegas Boulevard, Las Vegas, Nevada (on the far end of the Las Vegas Strip). It offers a large variety of dining choices and reasonably priced accommodations with all that you need on the premises, including a casino, shopping facilities, and a variety of endless entertainment.

There are two famous roller coasters to thrill visitors beyond their wildest imagination. The Canyon Blaster features four inversions: a double-loop and double-corkscrew that moves at 55 mph and is the only double-looped indoor coaster in the world. El Loco features 72 seconds of twist and turn droppings at 1.5 vertical-G, after ascending 90 feet. Both breathtaking rides will get your heart racing with their gravity-defying pulls, jumps, and drops and supply screams galore! Riders have to be more than 48 inches to ride these two magnificent creatures. Other ultra-thrilling and exciting extreme rides are The Inverter, Slingshot, and Chaos—with mind-blowing G-force action and whirling and flipping to make your head spin long after the rides.

The Theme park also provides magnificent traditional midway carnival games, video gaming arcades, and enjoyable family rides. The latest addition thrill ride is the NebulaZ—consisting of spinning arms that defy gravity-pull in all directions. There is also entertainment in the form of an FX theater with 4D features, a pirate ship ride, bumper cars, laser tags, mini golf, mini bowling, bungee jumping, rock climbing, and much more to discover. The venue will provide endless excitement for the young ones and nostalgia for the parents.

When you're ready to take a break, a circus act is a perfect option. The largest permanent circus area in the world hosts daily, free, world-class circus shows inside the retro-looking Circus Circus Casino hotel. Some of the best circus acts start at 11 a.m. daily, including trapeze artists, silk dancers, contortionists, jugglers, and clowns (of course!). They also light up into neon delight on the glow-in-the-dark weekend neon nights.

THE ADVENTUREDOME LOGISTICS

The AdventureDome is open daily (except on holidays), but operating times are subject to change or closure. It is recommended to view the updated schedules online or to call because daily time schedules apply, which are updated regularly according to seasonal changes. Hours generally range between 10 a.m. to 9 p.m. during the week and until midnight over the weekend. You have free entry to the theme park, but ride tickets have to be purchased. Individual ticket prices range between $5 and $12, and it is best to purchase (non-refundable) all-day passes, which entitle you to access unlimited rides. These are valid for one-day use only and can be purchased up to 45 days in advance. You need an ID or license to collect tickets that are bought online. They strictly enforce specific height requirements for individual rides. Rides for younger kids and family rides are also available. A regular pass requires measurements of 48 inches minimum at $60, and a junior pass for kids under 48 inches is sold at $30. (prices are accurate at the time of publication. Please check the Circus Circus website for current pricing.) Older kids taller than 48 inches can do the premium rides.

Various discount coupons are available. For example, Circus Circus Hotel guests receive a discounted price on their tickets. The hotel also offers Military, senior, and AAA discounts. Las Vegas and Nevada residents also qualify for discounts at the AdventureDome. Family-friendly options for youth groups (15 people or more) and packages offering ride bundles with discounted rates are also available. In addition, birthday party groups (these include themed catering and entertainment with party favors like decor and invites) can be arranged. Other promotions are regularly updated. Group arrangements can host events from 15 to 5,000 people.

With all the exciting rides and a wide variety of activities, plus generous and easy parking options, the AdventureDome provokes a certain trigger for lots of smiles and laughter.

THE ADVENTUREDOME ACTIVITIES

The Family Rides
Many exciting rides are available for various age groups, as well as games and rides suitable for the younger and more timid ones. Most of these rides can easily be found in the domed park after you have purchased your day pass ticket. Let's look at some of the favorites.

B.C. Bus

This ride is a mock bus ride over the hills! It offers a scenic view of the AdventureDome, from above when the bus hovers in midair for a short while before it continues to circle. This adventure bus (for the younger ones) goes up and down and round and round at a gentle pace, and kids have to be 36 inches to ride or be accompanied by an adult.

Drifters

Drifters is a Ferris wheel ride in the form of hot-air balloon passenger cars that will delight any fantasy. The ride provides a scenic experience and gently carries you up and away into dreamland, where you can see the AdventureDome from another angle. It's a fun and gentle experience, and kids must be 42 inches tall or accompanied by an adult.

Circus Carousel

No theme park is real without a traditional classic carousel ride. On this carousel, you can choose a fantasy ride on your favorite animal and gently go around to experience the flowing motion of the carousel. Riders have to be 42 inches minimum or accompanied by an adult.

Road Runner

The Road Runner is a mini-Himalayan box-car ride that goes forward or backward and offers exciting scenery while taking the younger kids on a slightly faster speed around and gently sloping up and down. Kids have to be 42 inches or taller or accompanied by an adult.

Frog Hopper

For those energetic little ones, the Frog Hopper is the ultimate ride that jumps up and down like a frog. This is a brilliant option for active little ones to get rid of all the pent-up energy of having to sit still while traveling to Las Vegas. It's an ideal ride for smaller kids. They stay seated securely, go up to mid-level height, and then jump down in a falling stop-and-go motion. And then repeat the jumping again—up, down, up, down! Kids must be between 36 and 58 inches to ride this jumping frog.

Thunderbirds

A more gentle ride with its flying motion in little vintage airplanes is the best ride for kids with delicate sensitivities. They can play pilot with a forward flying motion at an elevated position that gives a scenic experience. It consists of 1920s airplane cabins that go up and down while circling the centerpiece. Smaller kids between 36 and 58 inches will enjoy this ride.

The Entertainment

4D Theater

Experience special effects in the 4D theater with well-known animated characters. An added dimension of time and motion enhances the experience in the 4D theater. Two shows are currently available: Ice Age and SpongeBob SquarePants, and you can also enjoy an interactive ride experience with the Angry Birds characters.

The whole family will enjoy the interaction with Ice Age's saber-toothed squirrel, Scrat, who has to find and protect his nut (don't we all!?) in the screening of *No Time for Nuts*. He takes a time travel adventure with a time machine that destroys his beloved nut and is joined by his friends Diego, Manny, and Sid while you are taken on the ride in 4D motion. Or, if you prefer other character shows, you can take a treacherous ride against Plankton with SpongeBob to rescue Jellyfish as you whizz through an underwater adventure at Bikini Beach. For both exciting interactive adventures, you have to be 33 inches at least and accompanied by an adult. Be assured that adults enjoy this as much as kids!

The Extreme Ride Theater

In the Extreme Ride Theater—an interactive theater ride with contemporary shows and fantasy characters—you can have your heart pumping with excitement and action. Enjoy the simulator ride with some of your favorite action shows while your seat comes alive.

The VR Room

The entertainment at AdventureDome also includes a virtual reality room to take you to another extreme. There are ten games to distract you from the mundane reality into another world and a variety of additional games that suit every fancy.

The Circus Circus Show

Daily clown entertainment and circus shows are presented at the hotel for free. Don't we all love to smile at the quirks of clowning and gasp at acrobatic displays? Shows are held more than once daily, and additional shows occur over the weekend.

Neon Nights

Discover what Vegas is known for—its lights—and enjoy the extravagance of a glittering AdventureDome at night. Every Friday and Saturday night, the whole AdventureDome lights up into a glowing extravaganza with a magical touch. Video vibes include midway games, rides, and neon attractions, as well as face painting and t-shirts, all in the name of neon. The neon disco roller skating rink provides much fun and glowing laughter after dusk.

Treasure Island

OVERVIEW

The Treasure Island hotel is a Radisson hotel and world-class resort at the heart of the Vegas strip, offering a wide range of amenities. It provides spa facilities, live entertainment, an extensive 95,000-square-foot casino, themed attractions, 18 splendid dining facilities, exotic bars, cocktail lounges, and many more to maintain its four-star rating. The hotel has 2,448 rooms and 220 luxury suites, which were newly renovated between 2018 and 2020. It is close to many other luxurious Las Vegas resources and attractions, and the hotel offers a tram car facility for quick access to them.

Enjoy the full spa and salon treatments and 24/7 room service. Sip appetizing cocktails at the tropical oasis poolside under the palm trees, and even rent a private cabana. Find the ease of access to all amenities, enjoy fast internet, choose from a variety of luxurious dining options, and experience complete relaxation without having to go far. Once booked, the hotel has additional extras that can be purchased and a rewards program that adds some exclusive benefits to your stay. It also offers a snazzy Golden Circle Sportsbooks and Bar for Dad, with all its cool sports memorabilia, where he can grab a craft beer and watch his favorite game while the children have fun and Mom is shopping.

THE LOGISTICS

To make your visit to Las Vegas easier, The GO Las Vegas pass helps you save money, especially when your itinerary involves a variety of attractions. You can save up to 60% on more than 30 hotel attractions, including shows, tours, museums, and thrilling rides. The pass can be purchased on a choice- or day basis for up to seven choices or five days. With the choices pass, you can choose your specific attractions, while the day pass allows all-inclusive access to various attractions for the whole day. The most significant benefit of the pass is that you can download and purchase it online and thus skip the queues while the kids have to hang around.

The Treasure Island hotel is situated on the southwest corner of Spring Mountain at 3300 Las Vegas Boulevard South, Las Vegas, Nevada—opposite the famous Venetian resort and Grand Canal

Shoppes area and walking distance to the Fashion Show Mall. Easy, free self-parking is available from Mel Tormé Way, off Spring Mountain Road and the I-15 highway. Hotel check-in and check-out times are at 3 p.m. for arrival and 11 a.m. for departure, but changes can be arranged at an additional cost. The hotel also offers express self-check-in and check-out facilities. If you join their MyTI program and book using the MyTI TV promotion, the resort fee becomes optional. The resort fee gives you access to WiFi, the fitness center, and additional amenities. If you will not be using these features, being able to opt-out of the fee is a nice feature.

THE ACTIVITIES

Treasure Island's biggest attractions remain the Mystère show by Cirque du Soleil and the Marvel Avengers S.T.A.T.I.O.N. exhibit. These two main family attractions will surely supply all the joy and amazement that every family member needs to make a family vacation the most epic one of all.

Marvel Avengers S.T.A.T.I.O.N.
A visit to the Avengers S.T.A.T.I.O.N. will delight the whole family with an amazing interactive experience. The Scientific Training and Tactical Intelligence Operative Network is the full name of the acronym, and being interactive is the most amazing aspect of this venue. Visitors can engage in the cinematic universe of their heroes. The Marvel Universe exhibit displays the blockbuster film series *The Avengers* elements. Marvel in the fantasy of superheroes and interact with their experiments! A

visit to the public display of the superhero universe reveals the reason for the movie's success in a fun and lifelike exhibit.

All the main characters, the associated memorabilia, and the details of their victories will delight the whole family. You can experience the unique adventure of becoming a secret agent with its state-of-the-art equipment that includes top-secret files and classified studies. The adventure begins in a briefing room before you start, with an electronic introduction by Maria Hill, who heads up your interactive assessment at the S.T.A.T.I.O.N. venue. The exhibit displays an extensive range of items like the uniforms and shields worn by the superheroes, e.g., Captain America, Hulk, Thor, and many others. Participants can touch and activate the buttons for added fun and join in a fun interactive game at the end of the exhibit. You can become one of the Avengers heroes on the premises and join the fight in defense of the planet. Maria Hill encourages participants to participate in the interactive experience and offers access to the top-secret files and advanced science related to the superhero universe before she invites you to take on the challenge.

Your experience starts when you enter an 8,000-square-foot gift shop to purchase tickets. Always check for discounts and special deals that are regularly updated (e.g., Treasure Island guests can ask for a two-for-one entrance deal, group rates for ten or more guests, or special features and deals for private events). At the time of publication, tickets cost $40 for 12 years and older and $30 for ages 4–11 years. Children under 3 can enter for free. Operating hours are from Monday to Sunday between 11 a.m. to 6 p.m., with the last entry at 5 p.m. There are always queues, so be prepared for a bit of waiting and go early. Photos with your favorite characters (at an additional fee) can be taken here, or you can opt for a free photo in front of the show's main characters.

Mystère by Cirque Du Soleil

Mystère is the most phenomenal circus show on earth, and it makes a visit to Las Vegas your priority. The talented acrobatic cast plays with gravity in breathtaking dimensions. No challenge stops their human performance. The Cirque is known for taking on challenges that join a variety of disciplines never done before while they push the limits further. The majestic acrobatic shows are performed in water, on ice, with trampolines, teeter boards, straps, poles, trapezes, etc., and add heartwarming performances by clowns and fantastic tales to delight all ages in the audience. It further combines exquisite music performances and magical costumes. "Mystère™ is the original, must-see Cirque du Soleil® show that combines powerful athleticism, high-energy acrobatics, and inspiring imagery that has become the company's hallmark" (Treasure Island Las Vegas, n.d.). The show is held exclusively at Treasure Island, and it evokes the mystery of life as it mesmerizes and amuses the audience.

"It's a feast for the eyes that has completed nearly two decades of critically acclaimed performances" (thingstodoinlasvegas, 2016). Apart from many nominations and an array of awards, the show has received honorary awards as the "Best Production Show" nine times by the Las Vegas Review-Journal. It holds an international cast of 65 top-performing entertainers, including dancers, singers, acrobats, and musicians that delight the audience with a whimsical drama of mysteriousness and magical performances. It combines comedy, nostalgia, and excitement while interacting with the audience.

Any visitor to Las Vegas has to experience Cirque du Soleil simply because they will never be the same after watching these jaw-dropping magical performances. The show dives deep into your imagination with its unusual circus acts. After the show, you can step out of that "other universe" and try to convince your kids to not try the same acts at home! The show takes place in a magnificent 1,600-seat theater offering 90-minute shows daily at 7 p.m. and 9 p.m. as well as "dark date" shows on some Wednesdays and Thursdays. Ticket prices start at $225, and there are no age restrictions, although parents should be mindful that little ones may be frightened by some acts, the sound, and the darkness. A variety of promotions and discount coupons are available, including group and military discounts. Reservations can be made online or at the Box Office.

SkyPod

To take your vacation to another elevation level, you have to visit the STRAT Hotel, Casino, & SkyPod, which towers majestically at 800 feet above Las Vegas. Here you can feed your adrenaline appetite in midair with the most incredible views and attractions.

OVERVIEW

The SkyPod is an iconic fixture of the Vegas Skyline. The best views of Las Vegas are guaranteed, and some of the best attractions are as well! The SkyPod is "the tallest freestanding observation tower in the United States" (The STRAT Hotel, Casino & SkyPod, n.d.), and it towers above the glittering city at a staggering 1,149 feet. It is taller than the Sydney-, Eiffel-, and Tokyo towers and offers you some of the most colorful stratosphere sunsets. The venue offers a wide variety of dining and entertainment opportunities.

For fine dining culinary delights, you can feast in the elegant Top of the World revolving restaurant with its etiquette-styled ambiance. Other options include pizza or antipasto at Nunzio's Pizzeria or pub fare and craft beer at the sports bar. You can satisfy your thirst with your favorite coffee fix at Starbucks, a signature cocktail on a daybed, or a cabana at the Elation Pool and Café bar on the 8th floor. With so many choices, having a bite to eat will suit every craving and budget.

Entertainment shows include dance, magic, comedy, fantasy, mind reading, and much more. Families can also opt for show and dining packages. Apart from dining and entertainment, the variety of bars and lounges provide unforgettable settings, views, and designer cocktails. The 108 Drinks Bar is known for its iconic drinks, so enjoy some glamor while you unwind after a day filled with unforgettable activities. You can also SkyJump from this level if you are brave enough! SkyPod offers incredible observation decks at various levels and out-of-this-world thrill rides that are certainly not for the fainthearted... It is quite obvious that you cannot avoid a visit to the STRAT, filled with thrilling experiences and jaw-dropping amazement.

THE ACTIVITIES

The STRAT hotel includes some of the most extreme rides to get your adrenaline rush up to another level, namely the Big Shot, X-Scream, Insanity, and the very popular SkyJump freefall.

Observation Decks

The observation decks offer a 360-degree panoramic view of the city and the valley beyond. Indoor decks offer glass windows from floor to ceiling, and outdoor decks provide clear views (weather permitting) with viewfinders to zoom in on the detail of the city far below. From here, you can see helicopters at eye level and feel elevation exhilaration as you venture out of the troposphere into the stratosphere atmospheric level. Enjoy exquisite sunset views and the illuminating lights of glittering Vegas from an eagle's viewpoint. To enhance your experience, unwind in the eateries and lounges while watching others take part in the extreme thrill rides. At the time of publication, entry starts at $15—group discounts and also thrill ride packages are available with the SkyPod observation decks experience. The tower is situated slightly north of the Vegas Strip and Sahara Avenue intersection, and operating hours are from 10 a.m. to 1 a.m.

The Thrill Rides

Step outside into the stratosphere and experience some of the most extreme rides of your life! The Big Shot ride shoots straight up the mast from the 921-foot high platform of the tower at 45 mph for 160 feet in a matter of seconds and then down again for a nightmarish thrill. If shooting up and down a mast at 1,081 feet above ground does not provide enough excitement for you, then you can dangle out on the Insanity ride to view the bustling city at 866 feet below. The massive mechanical arm extends 64 feet over the SkyPod edge and spins the passengers in the open air at speeds that pull 3-Gs while simultaneously dangling them at a 70-degree angle and then tilting them straight down again. If you are brave enough, you may just be able to open your eyes to the view to tell the tale later! Because of the elevated position and high centrifugal force, riders have to be at least 52 inches tall, apart from the regular extreme ride requirements that can be seen on the ride's website. The third extreme ride is called the X-Scream. This roller coaster ride propels head first and then lets you dangle weightlessly from an elevated 866 feet above Las Vegas at 27 feet over the edge of the SkyPod. Then it pulls you back and repeats the propelling for more screams. Riders have to be 52 inches tall and be aware that the ride includes jarring motions (vertically and horizontally) at high elevations. Like Insanity and Big Shot, the ride is not for the fainthearted.

All three rides are subjected to suitable weather conditions. With these rides, you can catapult up to touch the sky while pulling four G's upwards and negative G's downwards as Big Shot makes you squirm. If you manage to catch your breath, you will be able to enjoy a bit of the view as well! Or dangle and spin from Insanity and X-Scream to remove all fears!

Operating times are Sunday to Saturday from 2 p.m. to 10 p.m. You have to be 15 years old to have a go, and younger riders have to be accompanied by an adult. Military and Nevada resident discounts apply, and at the time of publication, prices range between $29.00 (single ride) and $43.95 (unlimited rides), including a SkyPod admission pass. The high-speed ride at this level of elevation generates intense G-force pull and acceleration, so strict requirements apply, and riders should not suffer from any physical, medical, or mental conditions.

SkyJump

If controlled free-falling is more in line with your idea of adventure and adrenaline rush, then you can enjoy a SkyJump from the top of the tower that lunges you back to solid ground after an 855-foot drop. It is very similar to a vertical zip-lining experience. One reason why you have to do this is simply to tell your friends and have them watch while you take the leap!

Extremely strict rules apply before you can make this jump, so my advice is to peruse their website for details before you venture into this elation. You have to be in sound medical and mental condition, measure more than 52 inches, weigh less than 265 pounds, produce a valid ID, those between 14 and 17 years old must be accompanied by a legal guardian, and no jumps are allowed for individuals younger than 14 years.

The leap takes about 45 minutes to complete from the start of the preparation and multiple security checks. It is the only sky jump in North America and also the highest one worldwide. For extreme safety, the jumper is harnessed well and connected to a machine that guides the descent on course. Before reaching the ground, the jump speed is reduced to secure a safe and gentle landing. The activity is inspected daily (for security reasons) to guarantee its annual certification. It has been operative since 2010, with more than 200,000 jumps up to date.

Taking this jump will be a life-changing experience for all jumpers. The anticipation builds as you are geared up and wait for your trip up to the observation deck. From there, you will wait in a queue where you can see other jumpers taking their plunge. They take one person at a time into the room for the jump while other members of your group can watch through the window. A final check of your gear is done, and you are then directed to the platform, where another check is done as you are connected to the wires. Standing on the platform is where the height of adrenaline kicks in as well as all of the nerves. Once you are secured to the harness wires and all checks are completed, you are instructed to stand on the edge of the platform with your toes over the edge. They do a countdown, and then you jump! (Or just fall forward if you are like me and shaking too much to actually jump!) This is when you feel the full exhilaration of the experience. The views of the city are amazing, and you genuinely feel as if you are floating about the ground. There was no feeling of falling in the stomach or anywhere, and the only way to know you really were falling was to look down and see the ground getting closer to you. The whole drop takes just seconds, but it feels much longer as you just soak in the experience. Don't be surprised when you finally land that the first thing you say is, "That was so AMAZING; I want to do it again!" This is an experience that you and your family will talk about for years to come.

At the time of publication, operating hours are from Monday to Wednesday—2 p.m. to 10 p.m., Thursday—12 p.m. to 10 p.m., and Friday to Sunday—12 p.m. to 12 a.m. Prices start at $129.99 for the jump only up to $164.99, which includes photo or video footage. Discounts apply to STRAT Hotel guests and Nevada residents. Between 3 p.m. and 5 p.m. daily, you qualify for a free 'encouraging' drink from 108 Drinks and a 20% discount on the jump. (The shot can be substituted for a non-alcoholic option for those under 21 years.) Note that time slots fill up, so book your jump at least 1 month in advance. Also, note that jumps can be canceled if there are high winds for safety reasons, so plan your jump near the beginning of your trip so you have the ability to reschedule should your jump be canceled.

Takeaways

The most common tips for a pleasant visit to Vegas are mentioned below:

- Use public transport between places unless you want to walk yourself tired! They are further apart than you may think. Public transport is rated as medium safe, but it's wise to avoid public transport areas at night. There are also "hop on, hop off" buses you can purchase fare for a day to use.

- Wear comfortable shoes and clothes. Do not remove your shoes to walk barefoot in public places (for hygiene and safety reasons).

- Be mindful of the high Summer temperatures and rain. Get accurate forecasts a week before you arrive.

- Be safety conscious when you leave the boulevard and remain alert to the traffic. Many tourists are distracted while driving, or you may encounter intoxicated drivers.

- Keep to the main areas where cameras and increased police presence or patrolling are evident for your safety.

- Don't open doors to strangers in your accommodation. Avoid leaving valuables in open sight in your vehicle. Don't carry all your cash on you.

- Always keep your identification with you.

- Avoid street entertainers. They may entice you to pose for photos and then charge you exorbitant fees for that!

Next, we go to the mountains and forests of Tennessee!

Your Review Makes a World of Difference!
Share the Joy of Exploring Together

"The greatest adventures are shared ones." - Unknown Adventurer

Hey there, fellow explorers! I've got a super cool thing to tell you. Did you know that people who help others, just because they want to, end up being super happy and even luckier? That's right, and I want us to be the happiest, luckiest bunch of travelers out there!

So, I have a little favor to ask you...

Would you be willing to help someone you've never met? Someone just like you who loves going on awesome trips with their family but might not know where to start?

That's what "The Extraordinary Family Travel Guide, Bucket List USA" is all about! It's a special book that's all about helping families like yours discover the coolest, most amazing places in the USA. And guess what? You can help make this book a superstar!

Here's how it works. Most people decide which book to read based on what others say about it (yep, even adults do that!). So, I need your help to tell the world how much fun your family had planning trips with this book!

Please, help other families find their dream vacations by leaving a review. It won't cost you a penny and it's super quick – I promise!

Your review can help...

...another family get super excited about their next adventure

...other kids and parents discover the most fun places to visit

...everyone plan trips that are as unique as they are

...turn dream trips into real-life adventures!

To share the fun and help out, just click the link or scan this QR code and leave your review:

https://www.amazon.com/review/review-your-purchases/?asin=1960049003

If you're smiling thinking about helping someone you've never met, you're awesome! Welcome to our club of joyful travelers!

I can't wait to share more secret spots and fun tips for your family trips. You're going to love the surprises in the next chapters!

A huge thank you from me, Jacklene Conner, your travel buddy and guide. Let's keep making family trips unforgettable!

PS - Here's a cool tip: When you share something helpful with someone, they'll think you're the best! If you think this book is a treasure for other families, why not share it with them too? Let's spread the joy of traveling together!

Chapter 5
DESTINATION #3 TENNESSEE

> *I took a walk in the woods and came out taller than the trees.*
> —HENRY DAVID THOREAU

You simply have to go and find the magic in the Great Smoky Mountains National Park with its rolling hills. The green forests and their color burst of leaves in Fall, cascading and gurgling rivers, and deer and bears will stir the nature lover in you. For an "adventure dessert," you can take part in fun activities like zip-lining, hiking, camping, and stargazing. There are plenty of outdoor activities in this perfect color palette of nature. The National Park has evolved since 1934 into the largest protected area on the eastern side of the Rockies, situated on the US 441 Highway. It is also the most visited national park in America.

An added bonus is that it's not expensive (reasonably priced accommodation, grub, and activities), you make new friends easily, and there is plenty of music, dancing, and musical talent. Memphis and Nashville are well-known names in the music industry, especially the Blues and Country music communities, and there are many thriving musical venues and live shows. You will also find many museums that showcase the local musical talent and history. The people are heartwarming, as is their homemade recipes and delicious food—"Southern meals are meant to satisfy" (Kollar, 2017). This southern hospitality (that makes everyone feel welcome and loved by easily starting conversations or giving recommendations and guidance for places to visit), together with the area's richness in historical architectural landmarks and museums to discover, makes it a highly desirable place to be. You will soon follow the laid-back vibe of "no rushing through the day," take a breath and live in the present moment again. Tranquil Tennessee avoids stress!

With an average of 16 crimes per square mile (the national median is 26,9), you are now venturing to a safer area with the family (NeigborhoodScout, 2022). In this chapter, I will give you some exciting activities to do in Gatlinburg and Pigeon Forge. The mountains are waiting there for you!

Gatlinburg and Pigeon Forge

THE GATLINBURG OVERVIEW

When you see a town has a black bear management program on its information website, you know they value the safe cohabitation and protection of nature and its inhabitants. And you know that they make time to breathe—the perfect venue for a relaxing vacation! No wonder it has become one of the top-rated destinations in the USA, offering an array of outdoor activities, family attractions, peace and quiet, arts, and entertainment, including live shows. Take a leisurely four-hour drive to Cade's Cove (25 miles outside the entrance of the National Park) to spot wildlife like deer and black bears. There are 800 miles of hiking trails in the national park to explore; you can take a unique Chondola ride up to the top of Anakeesta mountain or walk the longest Skybridge in Northern America. The list of exciting activities is endless, and you will most certainly come back for more. Some people say the Smoky Mountains have an Alpine feel with a Tennessee touch.

"At Pigeon Forge, a moment can last a lifetime" (Pigeon Forge Department of Tourism, 2022). A few miles away, you will find the quaint sister city of Pigeon Forge at the foot of the Smoky

Mountains. The 'village' will keep the family entertained for days, with multiple attractions and amenities to discover. Play mini golf, ride go-karts, visit parks, enjoy live shows, relax in spas, visit craft shops and historic sites, get active with sports and tours, or even whitewater rafting for the adventurous ones! Or, if you prefer a pure encounter with nature (perhaps a bear or two or a delicate fireflies display), you can rent a cozy cabin in the mountains and relax in the tranquility of trees and murmuring streams.

Gatlinburg is the doorstep to the National Park and 33 miles southeast of Knoxville, where the US 321, 411, 418, and 441 routes meet. Coming from the north, continue on Tennessee Route 66 to the south, and you will first pass through Pigeon Forge on the US 441 and then into Gatlinburg. Or you can approach Gatlinburg from Maryville via US 321. All the interstate routes (I-40, I-75, I-81) heading to the area are connected to Route 66. When flying to the Smokies, you will land at McGhee Tyson Airport in Knoxville, which is 47 miles from Pigeon Forge. From here, I recommend getting a rental car to take you into the town, so you'll have transportation to get around to all of the area attractions. The Gatlinburg/Pigeon Forge airport is a mere seven miles outside Pigeon Forge.

A family visit is worth a visit simply to enjoy the blue skies again and experience the simplicity of laid-back country life. Or if the young ones crave some entertainment, you will be close enough to a variety of options to choose from. In Gatlinburg, the Kid's Trout Fishing Tournament is held annually to encourage youngsters to spend more time outdoors and make fishing a positive experience. It also celebrates Free Fishing Day. Besides, the changing of the seasonal foliage will mesmerize the whole family with its colorful display. Make sure to plan your vacation accordingly because you do not want to miss the beauty of the life of trees. The highest rainfall happens in December and because of the exquisite foliage palette, the best time to visit the area is during the mild temperatures of Fall. But at the Smokies, like with most mountains, every season has its charm—it all depends on your liking.

ACCOMMODATION IN GATLINBURG AND PIGEON FORGE

A public trolley system offers free transport around Gatlinburg and enables passengers to get easy access to most of their destinations in town while visiting. The exquisite scenery of waterfalls, crystalline streams, and forest drives entice many photographers to test their skills against nature's perfection. In Pigeon Forge, the 1830s Old Mill is one of the most popular historic sites and worth a visit; it also offers a restaurant that is rated as one of the best places to eat in the area. Always remember to ask for savings and special deals or discount coupons for the various attractions at all the venues. Many vacation package deals are also available. A huge selection of comfortable and unique accommodations is available in the area. Once you have decided in which town you prefer to stay, you will be able to reach all the amenities easily. There are some definite differences between the two when I compare the options. Gatlinburg offers the following:

- It is closer to the National Park. Depending on your vacation planning and intentions, it's wise to make up an itinerary of sites and then accommodate the family nearby if you prefer to travel less. (Some National Park sites are closer to Pigeon Forge.)

- Gatlinburg has incredible mountain views, and they can be seen from the Space Needle or the Gatlinburg Bypass.

- It is more compact and pedestrian-friendly, with a unique downtown area. But it also gets more crowded, so it may not be the easiest place to take a leisurely *promenade* with kids and strollers.

- This place is a hikers' paradise, so if your family is outdoors-oriented and adventurous, staying here may be more functional.

- Pigeon Forge prides itself on its vast selection of attractions and activities:

- Dinner, music, and theater shows entertain crowds abundantly. You may want to clone yourself to attend all of them.

- The Island entertainment and shopping area offers many *alfresco* dining opportunities and also hosts an incredible synchronized fountain display that the kids will enjoy watching.

- The best-reviewed theme park in the country, family-friendly Dollywood, is located in Pigeon Forge. It offers 40 rides, including roller coasters, together with the best southern hospitality, as well as local entertainment, crafts, and food.

- Most importantly, Pigeon Forge has a well-known family vacation reputation with all that it offers to the younger generation.

Options in the towns include chain hotel stays or family-owned B&B options, and both are very popular. Some places are more remote, offering secluded inns, lodges, cabins, cottages, and chalets typical of mountain getaways. Condos, camping options, and RV parks are also available. The most popular resort is probably Dollywood's DreamMore Resort and Spa (in Pigeon Forge), offering guests the unique, luxurious ambiance that only Dolly Parton could envisage. The resort offers not only a variety of premier amenities but also discounted packages that provide value-for-money vacation entertainment for the family. If you prefer to make memories next to a cozy fireplace in a wooden cabin with exotic mountain views, your list in the area is endless. Gatlinburg is known for the largest selection of mountain accommodation choices of any other American destination. No wonder these mountains receive about 12 million travelers annually!

THE MUST-DO'S IN GATLINBURG AND PIGEON FORGE

With such a wide selection of things to do for the young and older generation in the Gatlinburg and Pigeon Forge area, I have thinned it down to a few unique family-friendly experiences to help you plan your dream visit. I am sure that after creating some of the most unique memories at the Smokies, the whole family will want to return to make more epic ones.

For All

Anakeesta

Anakeesta is an award-winning outdoor theme park. Some kid-review comments about Anakeesta should be enough to convince you that the place is magical—"We were at the top of the trees" (Drannan, aged 8), "You have to be 70 pounds to ride the zipline. So I ate a Sundae" (Hector, aged 6), and "My favorite part was playing in the treehouse" (Lecy, aged 5), (Tennessee Department of Tourism, 2022). It's an outdoor adventure paradise that will thrill the child in everybody and is aptly named "the place of high ground" by the Cherokee nation.

Access to the scenic 70-acre mountain top park is via a gondola with the option of choosing an open-air four-seater chair ride, or a six-seater closed gondola cabin to reach the mountain summit. The Ridge Rambler Adventure vehicle is another option for those who prefer a "grounded" and scenic drive to the mountaintop, 600 feet above Gatlinburg (576 Parkway). You will have unlimited access to gondola rides on your day's journey and should prepare to spend at least two hours on top of the mountain. Prepare for activities and walking once you reach the top, and wear the appropriate gear. You do not want to spoil your adventurous spirit with the wrong shoes and clothes.

This mountaintop venue aims to delight young and old—nature lovers and entertainment seekers. You can enjoy a magical view of the majestic mountains and also relax with a refreshing drink or heartwarming fare on top of the world with the clouds. Kids can play on 'Willow,' the friendly 15-foot tree sculpture that is the well-known "keeper of the forest" (with an interesting history to discover), or cool off in the nature-themed splash pad and run around. Mom can do some souvenir shopping or enjoy the lush blooms of the botanical garden and bird life. Dad can let go on the award-winning zip-line adventure, the teens can enjoy a thrill ride on the Rail Runner mountain coaster on a single rail, and the whole family can walk along the canopy of treetops on the longest skywalk in North America. The spectacular treetop skywalk is more than 800 feet of 14 hanging bridges connected to the trees at 50–60 feet above the ground and offers a bird's-eye view of the trees. Don't let the kids jump unless you want to roar with fear!

The village on the mountaintop is a place filled with adventure and relaxation offerings that prides itself on the amount of laughter and excitement it creates with visitors. You can visit Blackbear Village. There is a Gem mine with fossil treasures, a treehouse challenge course (BearVenture or TreeVenture), and a level II Arboretum called Vista Gardens that focuses on advancing the study and conservation of trees. Children will enjoy the informative and educational aspect of the garden while listening to cascading water and playing musical garden chimes. The informative Memorial Forest Walk (which pays homage to the suffering of the 2016 Chimney Top II fires) provides relaxation for all. The Anavista tower initiates 360 degrees of the most spectacular views at an even more elevated angle. It's also possible to visit at night to enjoy the stars while sipping a beer beside the fire pit and listening to live music or during colder months for a completely different enchantment to spot the first snow.

Make sure to research group rates, special packages, and updated seasonal events before you go. Discounted rates are generally given to AAA holders, senior citizens, local residents, and military personnel. An annual pass is available, and an all-day general admission pass allows for unlimited access to everything on the day. Children under three enter for free.

Gatlinburg Craftsmen's Fair

This unique trade fair hosts masterful local craftsmen and artisans from all over the nation, who gather at the foot of the mountains to display their talents and products. Currently, 200 booths of uniquely handmade products of these skilled artists are displayed twice a year. Originality is the keyword here. The products are all sourced via a rigorous selection process to ensure that the products are of a high standard and distinctive to avoid duplication. It's a lively opportunity to shop for unique handmade products and watch live demonstrations by skilled artists. It was voted one of the "Most Popular Events" of the Southeast by the Tourism Society (Gatlinburg Craftsmen's Fair, n.d.). and "Artisans in nearly 400 fairs voted our Fair 5th All-Time Favorite Fair in the nation" (Gatlinburg Craftsmen's Fair, 2017b).

Some of the crafts you may find here are dream catchers, jewelry, book art, pressed flower artwork, masterful woodcraft, glass blowing, leather bags, fairytale dresses for little girls, handmade knitwear, unique pottery, copper art, holiday wreaths, candy-making, custom-made knives, Christmas ornaments, and more! The best option is to do your annual Christmas shopping here. The kid's corner during the July fair provides an opportunity for D.I.Y. products that the young ones can take home with them while Mom and Dad can enjoy some free live music on the premises that includes an eclectic range of Country, Bluegrass, and Gospel music talents.

The venue is at 920 Parkway, in downtown Gatlinburg at the Convention Center—at traffic light number 8. The Fair hosts its 47th anniversary this year (2022) and is usually held twice a year during Summer and Fall (mid-July and mid-October) with daily entry from 10 a.m. to 5 p.m. Kids under 17 years can enter free with a paying adult, and fees are nominal for a full day pass. Multi-Day passes are also available (and free!), and groups of 15 and more may ask for a discount.

Mountain Coasters

There are many mountain coaster rides in the area to take your thrill level up to another height. I suggest trying some of the following options: the Moonshine Mountain Coaster (formerly known as the Gatlinburg Coaster) and the Smoky Mountain Alpine Coaster. These adventure rides are safe, family-friendly rides that give you control of the ride with its brake handles while providing a lot of fun and laughter. You can manage the speed of the ride as gravity pulls you down the mountain, and the rides require no skill at all. All you need is a fair bit of common sense and safety knowledge. All the coasters vary in length, maximum speed, and solo- or dual riding. At the Rowdy

Bear Adventure Park (at Rowdy Bear Ridge in Pigeon Forge), you can add some thrill in the form of snow tubing, a Power Coaster, or the Laser Gun Coaster.

The Moonshine Mountain Coaster is located at 306 Parkway, Gatlinburg, at traffic light number 2, as you come into the town from Pigeon Forge. It was the first coaster ride in Gatlinburg and is rated as one of the best in the area. Some of the awards name their top-rated votes, first-place vote, second-place vote, and most-thrilling-ride votes. It was recently upgraded when it passed ownership, and extreme care was taken to upgrade the safety standards to the German manufacturer's (Wiegand) standards. The ride is 3,000 feet long, with an elevation drop of 250 feet, and the ride lasts about five minutes.

The Smoky Mountain Alpine Coaster is the longest ride in the area and is situated at 867 Wears Valley Road, Pigeon Forge. At traffic light number 3, you turn onto Wears Valley road as if heading toward Cade's Cove. The Smoky Mountain Alpine Coaster is a mile long, and the exhilarating ride lasts about eight minutes.

For mountain coaster rides, you will be taken up to the top of the ride via a lift or pulled up slowly in the sled while you can watch the scenery and maybe spot some wildlife as well. From there, you enjoy the thrilling downhill glide while you whizz through some of the most spectacular forests. At night time, the ride path is lit up with magical lights to give the experience a completely different exaltation. You have to measure at least 54 inches to operate the mountain coaster alone, but young children can be accompanied by an adult. Rides operate during all weather conditions, except for extreme rain and thunder conditions, and the coaster carries a limit of 350–375 pounds in weight, depending on the specific Mountain Coaster ride. (In wet conditions, this limit is reduced to 330–340 pounds.) The rider who controls the sled should be 16 years and older. Weight and height rules are strictly enforced for safety reasons, so I advise a perusal of each ride's guideline rules and regulations before attempting the thrill. People who undertake the ride should also be of sound medical and mental condition and be mindful of other users who operate the coasters simultaneously. Pregnant riders are not allowed.

Prepare to wear the appropriate attire for the ride—meaning closed shoes, shirts, and comfortable, active gear that fits well. No loose items or headgear are allowed, as these can hamper the safety and smoothness of the ride. Remember that you can reach speeds up to 35 mph, and you do not want to lose the hat you bought at the Craftsmen's Fair! Rates vary per individual and age group. The Smoky Mountain Ride operates from 10 a.m. to 11 p.m. and until midnight on Fridays and Saturdays. Tickets start at $6 (aged 3–6), $14 (aged 7–12), and $18 for adults. A second ride may be purchased at $10 after the first completed ride, and adults with Military ID pay only $16. The Moonshine Coaster rates are similar: $5 (kids from 3–7), $13 (youths of 8–12 years), and $17 (13 years up to adults). This ride offers many discounted specials, which can be found on their website. They also offer discounted re-ride rates and special packages for groups of over 20 people. Their operating hours are from 10 a.m. to 10 p.m. and until 11 p.m. on Fridays and Saturdays. Always remember to ask for discounted rates and group specials! All rates and operation times were correct at the time of publication. Verify with the location's website for current pricing.

Ripley's Penguin Playhouse

One of the top-rated penguin site destinations by *USA Today Travel* is a visit to Ripley's Penguin Playhouse, where a colony of Blackfooted penguins is hosted in a uniquely interactive exhibit of their natural habitat. It's a must-do at the famous Aquarium of the Smokies. Rated 2020 Travelers Choice by Tripadvisor and accredited by The Association of Zoos and Aquariums, this is a sure showstopper activity that will make the children aware of a very important change they can make to the environment.

You will find Ripley's at traffic light number 5 at 88 River Road, Gatlinburg. Once inside, a penguin camera gives free live visuals. There are also virtual tours, a glass-bottomed boat for lively close-up interaction, birthday parties, conservation programs, specialized events (e.g., Pancakes and Penguins), and quality time up close and personal with the penguins that are included in family programs and are regularly updated. The three most popular experiences with these lovable creatures include "pet, admire, and sleep" with them. A personal petting experience will give you expert penguin behavior advice, a photo, and petting. The PJ party allows you to spend a night with the penguins, which includes a scavenger hunt, a dive show, a continental breakfast, and a morning meeting with the penguins. For the creative ones, an artistic painting encounter can be arranged where you interactively help create a unique art piece with a cute waddling penguin that you can take home. This does include some real penguin footprint signatures! Prices for these at the time of publication range between $45 and $78 per person and are worth every cent!

If you would like to make the trip an educational one for the kids, a visit to the Playhouse is a must. Kids will not only be exposed to the joyous personal, and playful interaction with the penguins, but they will be able to learn more about the threatened species and how we can help to save them from extinction. Kids can crawl into see-through tunnels and watch the cute birds frolic, swim, and dive from an underwater viewpoint. The oldest penguin kid on the block was born in 1992. This 90s kid, called Jerry, likes to nap in the sun and wants his food to be served! You can view all the penguin profiles, each set up with a unique story and their names, on the *ripleyaquariums.com* website before you go to meet them in person.

Access is possible between 9 a.m. and 9 p.m. during the week and until 10 p.m. on weekends. Annual passes, individual passes, single attraction passes, and combo passes are available to suit every need—including unique experiences that cater to any educational or relaxing adventure. At the time of publication, fee structures range from $10 for small children (2–5 years), $20 for 6–11 years old, and $38 for adults (12 years and up). Kids aged 60 years and older will also find this interaction with the cute 'waddlers' invigorating!

Dollywood

Dollywood delights with similar thrills as Las Vegas but with a Southern charm that only a creative spirit could envisage. Owned by the famous Dolly Parton and Herschend Family Entertainment, Dollywood parks and resorts provide everything that every family member needs in one place: excitement, adventure, relaxation, luxury, beauty, and more! Tripadvisor rated Dollywood as the "Number One Theme Park in the United States" in 2022 (Dollywood, 2020):

At Dollywood, we celebrate the best of life as we light up the Smokies with rides, slides, music, food, and laughter—day and night. We invite you to our Tennessee home, where you can hold on tight to those you love most in the great outdoors in each beautiful season of the year.

You can find the resort at 2700 Dollywood Parks Boulevard, Pigeon Forge. (You are 200 miles from Nashville if the live shows entice you to extend a musical vacation...) Dollywood embraces the richness of the artistry and heritage of the Smoky Mountains. Apart from what you see, you will also feel the warmth of southern comfort and hospitality. Enjoy award-winning dining (more than 25 options to choose from), shopping experiences, top-rated live entertainment experiences, and fabulous shows (like the Dolly Parton's Stampede dinner attraction) while the kids embrace the excitement of one of the most exhilarating adventure parks including thrill rides (offering more than 50 thrill rides of a world-class standard, like the country's first wing-coaster ride called Wild Eagle) and lavish water park features. It offers a fair especially designed for kids called The Country Fair at Dollywood. It further hosts some of the largest festivals, where global music, food, dance, and art combine to thrill the senses. The family can also enjoy lavish accommodation at the DreamMore Resort and Spa, HeartSong Lodge and Resort, or for a different and more natural ambiance, at the Bear Cove Cabins with its spectacular views. You will need at least seven hours to spend at the park! Here, it is all about embracing love.

At the time of publication, a standard one-day pass will cost you $84 as an adult, and an array of packages and special offers are available to enjoy the "full monty"—like season passes, Stay and Play tickets, or tickets for more than one day. If you decide to stay for a few days longer, the fees are not much more. Seniors and children aged between 4 and 9 can apply for discounted tickets. Dollywood is open from late March until January.

For Teens

Breakout Games

For the latest trend in entertainment fun, the Breakout Games at 631 Parkway, Gatlinburg, offer enough to satisfy any inquisitive soul. This is the number one escape room game that keeps you occupied for a fast-paced 60 minutes before you can breathe again. If you ever wanted to be the hero, I recommend this immersive game of interactive fun. Each game brings unique challenges for you to solve. Groups of ten and more can apply for discounted rates. There are discounted rates of 10% off during the week, and prices range between $32 and $49 (at the time of publication), depending on the size of the group participants. Children under 14 years must be accompanied by an adult. This is a fun experience for teens with active minds.

These fun escape room games are basically structured and life-size games of twists and turns that give you clues to solve in a selected time frame to break out of a room. It's a wonderful way to unwind from reality in a group set-up and to build team rapport. Your team has to solve all the clues and puzzles for your escape plan before the time expires. The thrill is on to solve the mystery of the secret mansion or escape from a kidnapping... but make sure to never play this immersive game with people you do not know! Go ahead, crack the code that sets you free!

SMO Rafting

For a different kind of rafting experience than the one you had in the Grand Canyon, you can enjoy rafting on the Pigeon River in the Smokies. There are a variety of options to choose from. Most of them take on the river from their outposts at Hartford, which can be reached from exit #447 on the I-40 at Hartford road. SMO Rafting launches at #3299 and Rafting in the Smokies at #3595 on Hartford Road.

The SMO Rafting office is situated at 103 Silverbell Lane, Gatlinburg, and Rafting in the Smokies at 813 East Parkway, Gatlinburg. You will be surrounded by spectacular mountain scenery and the Cherokee National Forest on these trips while you trail through the rocky riverbed. The adventure will take approximately two hours, depending on your package, who you choose as your river outfitter, and the seasonal variables.

One of the oldest outfitters in the area (since 1978) is Rafting in the Smokies. They have assembled a team of certified and trained guides to offer sustainable, affordable, and safe fun on the river with their rafts. They are knowledgeable and enthusiastic about their rafting. SMO Rafting has been rated as the top outfitter for this adventure by Tripadvisor, where they received the Traveler's Choice Award after 5,000 guests reviewed them full 5-stars! The Upper River Trip was also named one of the Top Ten experiences in the US since its operations started in 1993. This family-owned business prides itself on delivering a fun experience with a high standard of safety measures. To experience thrilling rapids and incredible scenery with them, you can book a scenic float on Class I and II rapids (most popular with families and children of a younger age) or a Class III to IV Whitewater trip (catering for ages 8 and up). They also offer the longest trip on the river of 6,5 miles on their Upper Pigeon River Rafting Trip. SMO rafting offers trips that range from a gentle experience to extreme experiences with a smaller raft.

Because the river is dam controlled, the rafting usually takes place on Tuesdays, Wednesdays, Thursdays, and Saturdays. (The water levels are variable and unpredictable.) Bookings also depend on the season and vary accordingly, so it's best to peruse the websites for updated information. An array of group packages, vacation packages, and family packages are available that provide complete combo bundles designed for individual needs. They also offer additional adventures like zip-lining and ropes challenges. Check their websites for prices. Always ask for coupons and discounts.

Prepare for breathtaking scenery and epic adventures on the water! Also, arriving with the appropriate gear is essential— preferably a synthetic layering of clothes in cooler seasons that will dry quickly, shorts and swimsuits in Summer, and secure shoes. You also need to arrive with an extra set of clothes and a towel.

TITANIC Museum

Yes, there is a Titanic in the mountains! Its nostalgic legacy lives on in an exhibit at Pigeon Forge that will delight any age group. Many events are also held at the venue that hosts the world's largest Titanic museum attraction, located at 2134 Parkway, Pigeon Forge.

A permanent interactive display of more than 400 real artifacts can be seen at the museum. The experience goes beyond a mere exhibition by making the visitors feel like they are boarding the ship for a journey as real passengers, stepping back in time to 1912, with a complete boarding pass and all. This educational experience offers 22,000 square feet of history that honor the crew and passengers who lost their lives by sharing their individual stories with photographic displays of actual photos and precisely replicated galleries of the ship's interiors, including the grand stateroom. You can experience the true temperature of the water when the ship sank, also play on a 1900s Grand piano, experience the feeling on the lifeboat, walk the replica staircase, and take the captain's wheel on the bridge. You can enjoy first-class five-course dinners, kids can have scavenger hunts, even touch the tip of an iceberg, and take part in many era-specific events. It takes about two hours to gaze in wonder at the priceless treasures, stories, and exhibitions on the two decks of the replicated ship-shaped structure.

The most incredible LEGO replica of the Titanic is also displayed at the Pigeon Forge Museum. Consisting of 56,000 LEGO blocks and measuring 26 feet by 5 feet, it comes with a unique story of Brynjar Karl's journey that makes it worth a special visit (TitanicPigeonForge.com, n.d.-a).

A 10-year-old boy from ICELAND had a dream to build the World's Largest *Titanic* Model with LEGO® BRICKS. It was a daunting 11-month undertaking with his Autism. His inspiring story has generated wide media, where he shared his story in his own words.

His incredible masterpiece is housed and displayed as a featured attraction at the TITANIC Museum in Pigeon Forge. It's an exquisite display! Combo offers, military tickets, and group discounts are available. Opening times vary according to the season and can be found on their frequently updated time roster, but the museum is generally open all year between 9 a.m. and 7 p.m. during the week and until 8 p.m. over weekends. At the time of publication, kids under four years enter for free, tickets for kids between 4–12 years old start at $15, and adult tickets (13 and older) cost $35. Reduced rates are available if tickets are purchased online. There is also a family pass of $115 available.

Step back into some nostalgia and slow down!

For Kids

Arcade City

Children always love amusement parks, and Arcade City at The Island in Pigeon Forge (as well as Arcadia at Gatlinburg) offers more than enough excitement to keep the smiles coming. Arcade City is a modern family-friendly playing arcade with many gaming options and prizes for everyone, located at 131 The Island Drive, Pigeon Forge. Opening hours are from 10 a.m. to 11 p.m. Play cards range between $25 and $145 with reduced prices when purchasing tickets online.

Arcadia

In Gatlinburg, the kids can play their hearts out at the 25,000-square feet Arcadia amusement park with more than 100 games to choose from. Arcadia is situated at 115 Historic Nature Trail, Gatlinburg, just below the Space Needle in the city. The largest family fun center in the region abounds with activities, amusement games, and simulators, providing ample entertainment for young and old. Kids will find top trending games while parents can enjoy the nostalgia of pinball. At the time of publication, playing cards start at $10, ranging up to the favorite $100 playing card, which offers a $50 bonus.

Gatlinburg Skylift Park

The Gatlinburg Skylift Park offers a range of exciting attractions and scenery in the form of a lift, bridge, deck, center, and trail. It has the longest pedestrian suspension cable bridge (stretching a record-breaking 700 feet across the valley) in North America, 1800 feet above sea level! You will find this adventure heaven at

765 Parkway, in the heart of Gatlinburg, and it cannot be missed if you follow the yellow lift chairs!

Gatlinburg Skylift opened in 1954 and soon became a famous landmark as it transported visitors up to Crockett Mountain top for some of the best views in Gatlinburg. Today, the chairlift is an upgraded 3-seater with high safety standards and provides magnificent views while you venture to the top. Once you reach the summit, the Amphitheater Skydeck provides ample seating to relax while taking in the exquisite vistas. You can also walk on the trails and elevated boardwalk (offering a variety of viewpoints of the bridge), climb the 70 feet of Tulip Tower with its four elevated platforms for taking in the views, and enjoy refreshments afterward at the Center. This is a unique bucket list experience that you will remember forever.

The iconic Sky-bridge was completed on May 17, 2019, and since then has drawn many tourists to experience its swaying panoramic scenery of the majestic mountains and treetops 500 feet above Gatlinburg. The middle of the suspension bridge has a 30-foot glass-bottom section at the highest point to enhance the thrilling experience. While you are on top of the mountain, make sure to find out about events like live music shows that may be happening or take part in a sunrise walk with complimentary breakfast and coffee.

Opening hours are generally from 9 a.m. to 9 p.m. and until 10 p.m. in Summer, weather permitting. Shorter hours apply on Christmas Eve and Christmas Day. At the time of publication, prices range from $18–$36 depending on the type of ticket and age group. Single-visit or unlimited-visit tickets are available, as well as a SkyPass ticket that can be purchased online in advance to save money. Pensioners, local residents, and Military members get discounted rates. Groups and combo package prices also help to save money in your vacation budget.

Takeaways

A trip to Tennessee is the perfect combination vacation for a diverse family where the teenager has no patience for the needs of the ten years younger sibling, or vice versa, and Mom and Dad simply want to relax while the kids have fun…

From a little bit of nature combined with games and fun, we now travel to pure natural wonder and amazement in Wyoming!

Chapter 6
DESTINATION #4
WYOMING

The mountains are calling, and I must go
–John Muir

Photo by Austin Farrington on Unsplash

In this chapter, we will immerse ourselves completely in the mysterious power of nature. I will give you more information on one of the most popular national parks in the United States—Yellowstone National Park.

Yellowstone National Park

OVERVIEW

Yellowstone is the oldest National Park in the US and also the world's first national park. Here you can take the family for a memorable experience of all the senses where sight and sound overwhelm in all nature's glory. It is sometimes called the "American Serengeti" and is world-renowned for its unique geothermal activity, characteristic wildlife, and breathtaking landscape, including lakes, rivers, and mountain ranges. It is home to a dormant supervolcano called the Yellowstone Caldera. More than half of the world's geysers and hydrothermal activity (fueled by volcanic activity) are located in the park. The park was named a UNESCO world heritage site in 1978 and receives more than four million visitors annually. The 'out-of worldly' and fictional-feeling legendary place still surprises scientists, geologists, historians, and archaeologists who revel in the mysteries that the area keeps producing after millions of years of evolution. The heat below the surface creates an almost apocalyptic image when it connects with the cooler temperature above.

Yellowstone National Park is situated in the northwestern corner of Wyoming. Entry fees are $20 (entry on foot, bike, or ski) or $30 (motorcycle and snowmobile) and $35 (private vehicle) for visitors older than 16 years, and this fee provides a 7-day entry permit. Annual passes, lifetime passes, military passes, or senior pass tickets are also available. The park has five entrances with varying opening time schedules, depending on weather and seasonal conditions, as well as annual road maintenance. Your closest commercial airports (servicing Yellowstone) are at Cody and Jackson in Wyoming, Billings, and Bozeman in Montana, and in Idaho at Idaho Falls. Montana airport is serviced during the Summer months from Salt Lake City, Utah. There is a Winter airport shuttle service available between Bozeman and Yellowstone, but no public transport in the park, and a vehicle is required to navigate the vast area. A good option is to book a guided tour which will also enhance your experience by seeing the best of the park.

Let me try to pin down some of the main reasons why this magnificent park should be on your bucket list:

- It covers an area larger than combined Delaware and Rhode Island—2,219,791 acres (almost 3,500 square miles)—of exquisitely contrasting landscapes.

- The largest and oldest bison herd can be found here. Today the bison number a miraculous 5,000 after being threatened with extinction.

- The park, although mostly known for its bison and gray wolves, protects a diverse selection of wildlife. Moose, elk, pronghorn, two bear species, an additional 67 kinds of mammals, 5 amphibian species, 16 fish species, and 322 species of birds all live in ecological harmony together.

- It is a botanical haven of biodiversity. It is the largest megafauna location in the world.
- You will find more than 1,100 indigenous plant species, as well as 200 kinds of exotic plants and more than 400 species of thermophiles (heat-loving bacteria).
- The largest lake at a high elevation in North America can be found here. Yellowstone Lake is a grand dame of 132 square miles at an altitude of 7,731 feet.
- The park has an exquisite array of aquatic features. You will find more than 290 cascading waterfalls, and each is more impressive than the other. The Lower Falls of the Yellowstone River amazes viewers, with its 308 feet dropping at twice the height of Niagara Falls.
- The nine visitor centers in the park offer a multitude of knowledge and information.
- Apart from the wildlife and fantastic natural habitat of these animals, the most extraordinary feature of the park is its geological system. It has one of the largest calderas in the world, with more than 10,000 thermal features and over 300 natural geysers. The geothermal activity is astounding and will captivate all age groups.
- It also has one of the largest petrified forests in the world.

- The seasonal changes are extreme and thus produce unique experiences with every change in the climate. Winter has its own powerful solitude; while Spring brims with fresh life, wild weather, and roaring waterfalls; and Fall hums with activity before the dormant period starts. Summer draws most of the crowds…

- Here you will find the language of nature as bison rut in mating season, water defrosts in a sound journey after Winter, hungry bears awaken after months of Winter sleep, frogs come alive in chorus at sunset, the elk's high-pitched bugle calls for a mate, and of course the announcements of the howling wolves.

GUIDED TOURS OF YELLOWSTONE

It is crucial to plan your trip well if you intend to visit the park on your own. The huge area that it covers incorporates a multitude of attractions and long distances of traveling between them. I would advise a guided tour (of which there are many available) to make this trip more relaxing for the whole family.

Benefits
The obvious benefits of a tour are that the guides frequent the area often and they are familiar with seasonal differences and the most popular sites to visit. They also know where to find specific wildlife and will be able to improve your chances of spotting them. Spending at least one full day with a tour guide

will offer you more than a mere trip in the family car—with Dad having to concentrate behind the steering wheel and Mom having to keep the young ones occupied and content! You will be able to sit back and enjoy the scenery. Taking a multi-day guided tour is even better.

Logistics

Some of the best Yellowstone tours depart from Jackson Hole, WY, and some tours include packages that also take you to Grand Teton, where you can do two parks in one trip. For me, the best option remains to focus on Yellowstone only and take the time to take it all in for a few days. The park's diversity simply offers too much for a quick race right through it. Your chances of spotting wildlife are also higher in the early morning. A day trip will whizz you to the main sites, but an extended tour of more than two days will offer the widest selection of wildlife spotting and scenic experiences. Always prepare for extreme and sudden weather changes and dress according to the planned activity and seasons. It's advisable to always have layers of clothing in the Park since the weather is very unpredictable. The temperature also decreases with higher altitudes.

The Timing of the Tour

It is important to determine your preferences for seasonal changes when planning your trip, depending on what sites you intend to visit. In addition to this, you also have to consider the distance between sites and travel times associated with this. Just like the Grand Canyon trip, you may have to enter from a specific gate in order to get to specific sites timeously and have enough time at each of them. You simply cannot tackle Yellowstone without an itinerary because you will be very disappointed when you end up spending all your time only in the vehicle. Also, make enough time for walking the trails, having a picnic, or simply sitting patiently watching the wildlife crossing the road. Some hours of the day (like the twilight hours) evoke a very special atmosphere and should not be missed.

Available Types of Tours

A variety of guided tours are available and can easily be sourced through your travel agent or online. These include day tours, small group tours, private tours, cultural history tours, ecological tours, or longer tours. Some tours focus on the Lower Loop, others on the Upper Loop, and some are combined. There are main Yellowstone highlights tours, wildlife tours, and Yellowstone and Grand Teton combined tours. Others are specialized tours for those who want to experience Yellowstone off-the-beaten-track: a Kayak tour on the lake, a Winter day tour (snowcoach/snowmobile), a Winter hiking or biking tour, horseback riding tours, wildlife viewing tours, or rafting tours. I will highlight some of these, but the choice ultimately depends on your specific itinerary and family dynamics.

Unique Guided Tours

Guided tours for individual needs offer amazing packages in Yellowstone. Whether they happen on land or water, they are adventurous journeys that will linger for many years in your memory.

Boat

With all the water features present in Yellowstone, it is quite obvious that water tours will attract selective participants. There are gentle river cruises, exciting rafting tours, or serene kayak experiences on Alpine lake. These tour packages offer the best scenery while you experience nature from a closer angle. Some of them include glorious dining opportunities as well.

- Sightseeing charter boats offer scenic cruises (more or less two-hour trips) on Yellowstone lake, or you can take the Lake Queen boat for a scenic one-hour guided tour. From this scenic view, you will spot eagles and wildlife as you pass the shores.

- Another scenic float on the Yellowstone River is a family-friendly rafting option for younger kids, where you can gently glide down the river and experience a few rapids. The guides are knowledgeable about water safety, and you will spot some wildlife and finish the two-hour trip with smiles on your faces and hearts.

- A more intense full-day rafting trip that lasts about five hours and includes a picnic meal is perfect for families with older children and a more spirited mindset. You have to be physically stronger to take on the Class II and III rapids and the 18-mile endurance of the river. Wildlife can also be seen on this boat trip.

- Believe me—there is nothing as blissful and serene as a kayak trip in nature with only you, landscape, and silence. It's a definite must-do before you are too old! At Yellowstone, there are various kayak tour options available, and all of them allow escape from the busy crowds in the park. Moderate fitness levels are necessary for some of these trips, but some also accommodate small children who can sit on the parent's lap. Many of the trip options start early in the day (there is even a twilight kayak tour!) and take you to see some of the geothermal activity along the banks as well as below the water's surface. Prepare for some paddling and splashing that makes you forget about civilization for at least three to six hours! A private kayak tour will customize the experience to your liking and offer a gourmet picnic with unforgettable scenery.

Horse

"Horses have a way of making us feel unstressed" (Rockin' HK Outfitters, 2022). One of the most popular things to do in Yellowstone is horseback riding. An even more important horse-riding experience is to take the stagecoach adventure while watching the wildlife. These trips relive the pioneering stagecoach era of the Wild West on a partial-day tour. The park also offers an opportunity to take a canvas-covered wagon drawn by two horses, true pioneer style, out to your Old West Dinner Cookout venue under the magnificent stars.

There is a maze of horseback-riding tours available with a variety of options to suit every individual need. They vary from one-hour pony rides to simple two-hour riding trips to full excursions that cover multiple days in nature and overnight packages. (Some even combine rafting and horseback riding or trout fishing and horseback riding in one package.) The Yellowstone Mountain Guides Horseback Trailrides offer half-day as well as full-day rides to enjoy the scenery while clip-clopping along with the horses' hooves. Their horses and mules are gentle and surefooted, and they provide a safe experience for young and old. Prices range from $100–$395 per person, depending on the package and duration. They offer a sack lunch and water for the duration of the ride. Whichever option you choose, the tranquility of being one with nature while you trust your horse to carry you away from all your rushed thoughts is an unsurpassable experience.

It's important to wear long trousers and closed shoes when embarking on a scenic equine experience.

Private Transportation

Year-round private tours are offered at Yellowstone, and they are currently very popular. In this way, you can see most of the popular sites on the Lower Loop in one day with your family. Some private tours also offer the Upper Loop sites. The benefit of a private tour is that you can customize the itinerary according to your needs. This is the perfect option for Yellowstone visitors who have been there before and want to delight in a quick visit to all the famous landmarks of the area. *Viator* offers a big selection of options to choose from if private transportation through Yellowstone is your way to go.

Extra Tours

Mammoth

A full-day Grand Canyon Day Tour departs from the Mammoth Hotel and delights with a scenic adventure drive to the Grand Canyon of Yellowstone Park. The journey takes place mainly between Norris and Mammoth, and you will arrive at the canyon at midday, where you can leisurely spend two hours of sightseeing before the tour returns to Mammoth just before the day ends. It also includes a pre-packed lunch box (order the night before!), and you are encouraged to take your own thermos for hot beverages. They promise to make plenty of stops to view the wildlife. Rates at the time of publication are $124,50 for children (3–11 years) and $249 for adults. The tour starts at 8:30 a.m. and takes place on Mondays, Wednesdays, and Fridays.

Mammoth Hot Springs is a magical site for Winter tours. A wide variety of specialized adventure tours during Winter create a frosty wonderland of adventure with a completely different feel from here. Ski tours and shuttles operate daily to drop off adventurous skiers on Yellowstone ski slopes (only recommended for experienced skiers), but expert guides can also take other levels of skiers on a customized tour to some of the Winter wonder ski trails in the area. (You do need some skiing background to take part in these tours). Apart from ski tours, various sightseeing tours to spot the 'frost-coated' wildlife, gaze at trillions of stars, be mystified at the heated thermal steam in the low Winter temperatures, or simply gape at the wondrous soundscapes of the Winter landscape can be arranged from here.

The Norris Geyser Basin tour is another fascinating half-day Winter secret. This geyser is the hottest, has the most diverse water chemistry, and is the most acidic thermal feature in Yellowstone. In addition to this, it is also the most unpredictable (with temperatures above 200°F), so what you see today, you may not see tomorrow. You will have to do some strenuous walking in the snow to experience this colorful, magical sight, but it is truly worth the effort. (Rates at the time of publication are from $55 and $110, and the tour starts just after midday.) Whatever your family dynamics allow, there are enough options to choose from to satisfy your vacation spirit!

Old Faithful

A tour to watch some of the most prominent geysers of Yellowstone happens between Old Faithful and Madison. The area is called the Fire Hole and is known as the "heart of the greatest geyser region on Planet Earth" (Yellowstone National Park Lodges, 2017a). On this tour, the historic Yellow Bus takes visitors on an hour-and-a-half trip to the thermal areas. Wildlife can also be spotted on the way, and this is a highly informative evening tour. The tour starts at Old Faithful Inn daily, and rates at the time of publication range between $16.50 for kids and $33 for adults. The Yellow Bus returns you at 6 p.m. to spend the evening chatting away about all the thermal phenomena of the area!

Sunset Tour

An exquisite sunset tour can be arranged from the Lake Yellowstone Hotel with the old Yellow Bus. The Lake Butte Sunset Tour promises to deliver outstanding vistas, ample wildlife spotting, and a charming play of light effects as the sun sets. The driver of the bus takes all the details of this weekly (and constantly changing) journey into consideration while taking visitors to the viewing point on the summit of Lake Butte (at 8,348-foot elevation) to arrive just in time for the best sunset vistas. You will be able to see 360 degrees views, including Mount Washburn, Electric Peak, and Grand Tetons toward the South, all weather permitting, of course. Rates are $22.50 for kids aged 3–11 and $45 for adults. The pickup time varies according to seasonal changes and the sunset hour, but it's usually a little more than a two-hour scenic drive.

ACCOMMODATION

The two most popular lodgings in the park have deeply rooted historical significance.

Old Faithful Inn

This historical wooden lodge, built from local wood and stone in 1903/1904, is the largest log structure in the world. It features a massive fireplace made from stone, and a unique hand-crafted copper, wood, and wrought-iron clock. It is also the most popular lodge in the park.

Lake Yellowstone Hotel

Built-in 1891, this is the oldest lodge in Yellowstone, and bookings have to be made at least a year in advance. It has a completely different feel than the Inn with its Colonial heritage. It accommodates you in classic elegance. It recently received a National Historic Landmark designation, as well as a Green Seal Lodging Certification award for sustainability.

MUST-DO'S IN YELLOWSTONE

The park is so vast and offers so much to do that it is quite a challenge to take it all in. Don't try to rush through this adventure. It deserves your contemplative attention. I personally think the next few things are the most important attractions to visit in Yellowstone.

For All

Hayden Valley

Despite the "bison jams" and scores of tourists on the only public road through Hayden Valley, this scenic landscape is an absolute must-see. As for any wildlife viewing, my advice is to go early or later in the day to spot most of their activity. However, in Hayden Valley, you will not be disappointed, and the bison herds do roam the valley! The valley is centrally located in Yellowstone Park on the western side of the Yellowstone River and makes up about 50 square miles of the park.

It's a marsh-like broad valley containing lake sediments covered with glacial tills which remained after the previous glacial movement—13,000 years ago! Apart from the multitude of bison, you will definitely see other wildlife here. Space allows for majestic viewing, so have your binoculars ready. The elk and grizzly bears love it here, and you will also find abundant aquatic bird life because of the river's proximity. Smaller mammals, coyotes, and wolves may also appear at the right times of the day. Although there are some geothermal geysers in the Hayden Valley, they are not the main attraction. Visitors gather here to see wildlife. And so should you!

Yellowstone Lake

The largest high-elevation lake in North America is sure to attract attention. It's a haven for aquatic birds like the rare trumpeter swan, Canadian geese, loons, pelicans, cranes, and ducks. The lake is situated in the lower parts of the park, and the East entrance from Cody, WY, is the closest entrance to the lake. During Winter, the lake freezes completely, which leaves the water temperature too cold (41°F) for swimming during Summer. This is why it's advisable to book a boat trip on the lake so you can explore the vastness of the 141 miles of shoreline from a different angle. The 132-square miles of the lake covers an area of roughly 20 by 14 miles (plus an average depth of 140 feet) of sheer water that dazzles with its seasonal colors.

Fishing is also a popular sport at the lake, and Yellowstone is a fly-fishing paradise with its wide variety of game fish. The lake has the largest wild cutthroat trout population in North America, a very puzzling matter in particular to its distance from the sea... A further mystery of the lake is the underwater thermal activity that takes place below the surface. However you look at it, Yellowstone Lake is rife with historical and geological information waiting to be explored. Kayak tours on the lake are bountiful and offer packages to suit every family's needs. Although it's possible to enjoy the lake (and maybe a lazy lunch at the historic Lake Yellowstone Hotel) in a few hours, my advice is to stay for at least a day to absorb the aquatic ambiance.

Watch the Bison Roam

No other place on earth presents the same spectacular show of herds of Bison roaming freely. The plain sight of this is enough to produce goosebumps when considering that they were nearly extinct a couple of years ago after extreme hunting and poaching practices during previous centuries. Their saving grace was officially introduced with a law that prohibited hunting them in 1894, and their numbers gained a steady growth—from millions down to 25 in 1901 and back to about 5000 at present in Yellowstone alone. These huge 2,000-pound behemoths are the largest land mammal in North America and were voted the national mammal in 2016.

It's an undeniable thrill to see the herds roaming mostly in the Lamar and Hayden Valleys of Yellowstone. They are unpredictable and can run fast if they have to, up to three times the speed of an average human, so don't be fooled by their sheer size and tranquil demeanor while they graze or cross the roads! The chances are good to spot many of them if you take one of the many Yellowstone sightseeing tours. The best wildlife spotting time is always at dawn. In late Spring, you may even see some babies when the bison calf (between April and July), and soon after that, you can prepare for the annual bison rut when the bulls showcase their peculiar power and dominance.

Wildlife Watching

If you are short on time, the most promising way to see wildlife is through the trained eye of a wildlife coach tour. Jess Haas, the program director for the Yellowstone Forever Institute, summarizes the wildlife-watching activity so eloquently when she says: "No matter what kind of day you're having, a great wildlife sighting makes it better. It doesn't matter what kind of animal it is—a bear, a bison, a wolf—it just lifts your spirits" (Clark, 2017).

Lamar Valley, in the northeast corner of the park, is the most abundant wildlife spotting part—mainly because of the wide open spaces.

There are generally two ways of wildlife spotting: the wait-and-see approach or driving until you find a traffic jam of cars, and be sure to find the animals there! In Yellowstone, tours can be arranged with a knowledgeable guide who will take you with the refurbished 1937 Yellow Bus (departing from Mammoth Hot Springs as early as 6:30 a.m.) to spot most types of wildlife—coyote, mountain goats, bears, moose, hawks, osprey, and also wolves. The wolves are high on the wish list of wildlife spotting after their reintroduction to the park in 1995 after 70 years of absence.

For Teens

Grand Prismatic Spring

A "Football Field on Steroids" (Peglar, 2017) is probably the best description for this mega wonder. It is also the busiest area of the park and the most popular place to visit in the park. It doesn't take much explanation why—a mere glance at the surreal most-photographed thermal feature in Yellowstone all over the internet will be enough encouragement to make the journey despite the crowds. The spring is situated in the Midway Geyser basin of Yellowstone, in the northwestern area of the park, adjacent to Yellowstone lake. The precise coordinates are 44.5250489°N and 110.83819°W.

Keep in mind that you may not have a bird's eye view of the unique wonder like it shows in the photos; however, you will still be stunned by the mysterious play of water and light. The best time to see this is on a sunny day after the morning steam has evaporated. Let me try to highlight a few reasons why this place is so remarkable:

- It's the largest hot spring in the US and the third largest in the world.
- It is 370 feet in diameter and 160 feet deep (which is deeper than a 10-story building). 560 US gallons of boiling water (160°F) are discharged every minute.
- A fun fact to know is that anything that drops down the water can not be retrieved! So hold on to your hat while walking on the boardwalk and be mindful of its ecological sensitivity.

- The prismatic colors closely match those of a bright rainbow. The colors are produced by millions of heat-loving bacteria (thermophiles) that thrive in the outer layers of the spring's cooler water (showing their vivid green to red hues), while the sterile water of the deep center creates the blue hues as it plays with light reflection.

- The most extraordinary aspect of this spring is its forensic and scientific value. These living microbes in the water have helped to solve crimes, assisted NASA with extraterrestrial research, and produced incredible medical and scientific advancements. It helped to explain the human genome sequencing and was instrumental in recent research that led to the development of the Covid-19 PCR test. The water is basically a live thermometer!

Apart from this main attraction, a walk along the boardwalk will also produce more geysers to gape at and enjoy. If you do not come with one of the popular tours in the spring, you may need at least two hours to absorb it all as part of the crowds. You can also take a 60-minute round-trip hike to the new elevated viewing platform for a more aerial experience. It's a 1.2-mile moderate hike.

Old Faithful Geyser

This geyser has erupted more than a million times since the opening of Yellowstone park and is by far the most famous and predictable geyser to go and see. The geyser is situated in the southwest section of the park in the Upper Geyser Basin.

The eruptions take place about 20 times daily, every 60–100 minutes, when the geyser sprays its water up to 180 feet up into the air, lasting between almost two and five minutes. The predictions are very accurate at a 90% correct prediction rate and have been recorded since the park's beginning. These eruptions can produce up to 8,400 gallons of water during longer eruptions. It's surrounded by a fragile crust and very hot, with temperatures reaching up to 204°F and the steam even more at 350°F! Competing for the best view in the crowds can be quite challenging, but even from your worst position, you will still have an extraordinary experience of all your senses. (Arriving a few minutes before the predicted eruption time may secure you a front-row seat!) Quieter viewing times happen in the Winter months and before midday. There is also a visitor center and shops close by to spend some time while you wait for the eruption.

For Kids

Boiling River

If you like the attraction of opposites, having a "swim" in the Boiling River during Winter is a sure winner! Other seasons are also interesting, but for me, nothing awakens the spirit as much as bathing in a natural hot tub in freezing temperatures, whether you are young or old! This specific spot is not very well-known to tourists and is a rare find in Yellowstone, where swimming is not always possible. It remains a hidden gem tucked away within ten kilometers from the North entrance of Yellowstone (very close to the Wyoming and Montana border from Gardiner) en route to Mammoth Hot Springs. You will also cross the 45th latitude parallel (which is the midway between the North Pole and the Equator) for an additional memorable photoshoot!

A large hot spring enters the river at this point, and the waters mingle in the Gardner Mountain River to create a magical warm delight of between 100–140°F. It's important to obey the park rules and stay in the designated area for your own safety. The heat source can be very hot if you venture away from the safe shallow bathing area. It's also advisable to keep your head above water and not inhale too much of the thermal steam. You need about an hour for the experience, and your legs have to work a little (about ten minutes, but it's an easy walk for young kids) before they can relax in hot water. In Spring, the trails are closed when the river becomes too wild from the melting ice. The river is thus mainly open to the public from late Summer to the end of Winter. To enjoy the spectacular scenery of the mountain from the river, you have to wear water shoes for your safety and remember that the 'tub' is in the heart of nature with no places to change into bathing suits!

Junior Ranger Program

Of course, all kids want that honorable Yellowstone Ranger badge to show their mates at school after their most awesome vacation! These ranger programs are aimed at 4 to 13-year-old kids. The activities take place in the park, and the booklets can be obtained online or at visitor centers. There are three Junior Ranger programs (ages 4–7, 8–12, and 13 and up) with age-specific activities, as well as a specific Winter program booklet. With the booklet, the kids tick off specified things on the list as the family tours through Yellowstone, and they have to at least go on a hike and attend one ranger talk to get the highly valued Junior Ranger patch.

In addition, they can complete another set of activities, at an additional small fee, by taking part in the Young Scientist Program (aimed at children aged between 5–13 years). To earn this badge (and key chain for older kids above 14 years), the 10 to 13-year-olds have to complete two explorations. One is found at the Canyon Visitor Education Center, and the other one is at the Old Faithful Visitor Center. Specific Scientist Ranger program packets for the 5 to 9-year-olds can be obtained from Old Faithful Visitor Center. After this, they will be proud to showcase their Ranger Power!

Lamar Valley

As with Hayden Valley, this remote section of the park offers some of the country's most abundant and easily spotted wildlife. The park's most famous creatures found here are the magnificent wolf packs. The valley is tucked along the Lamar River in the northeastern corner of Yellowstone, about a 70-mile drive from Old Faithful. Apart from the magnificent wolves, you will also see all the other wildlife that frequents the rest of the park here at Lamar Valley. It also offers some of the most spectacular landscapes in the park and rings the Serengeti bell with its vast African-like savanna landscapes and mountain backdrops. You can also book two-day or four-day guided Yellowstone tours that include an extensive visit to the area. These valleys, where the wildlife roams so freely, produce deep serenity within.

Takeaways

- Be prepared for hiking, driving long distances, and extreme seasonal weather conditions when packing your gear for the trip.

- Don't forget your camera and binoculars!

- Bring hats and sunblock protection in Summer and appropriate warm clothes for Winter months.

- Never hike alone and make a bit of noise when hiking to alert the bears... Carry bear spray for an emergency and back off slowly when you encounter one. Don't run!

- Although the thermal systems may look very enticing, they are not meant for swimming or touching. Unless you want to get boiled, of course...

- Be mindful of wild animals and always respect the distances to maintain between you and them—a minimum of 25 yards from most wildlife and 100 yards from bears and wolves. After all, the park belongs to them!

- Bring bug repellent to make your life more comfortable: mosquitoes also love Yellowstone!

I think to truly experience Yellowstone (or any wildlife adventure) with all its visual, olfactory, and auditory sensations—it is necessary to stay over for at least one night. A

day trip to some of its unique attractions is not enough. You want to hear the wolves howl, don't you? From here, we make our last epic journey to Washington, D.C.

Chapter 7

DESTINATION #5 WASHINGTON D.C.

> *Washington, D.C., has everything that Rome, Paris, and London have in the way of great architecture – great power bases. Washington has obelisks and pyramids and underground tunnels and great art and a whole shadow world that we really don't see.*
> –DAN BROWN

Photo by Chris Hardy on Unsplash

For a family with older kids and/or teens, Washington, D.C. is a must-do. It's a combination between education and fun.

especially if you use the tricycles or segways as your transport through the National Mall. If history is your forté, you cannot miss a visit to The National Mall. Let me highlight the best places to see in Washington, D.C.

The National Mall

"I have a dream," said Martin Luther King Jr. in his famous speech from the steps of the Lincoln Memorial. Once you observe the U.S. Capitol Building, the Smithsonian museums, and the iconic architecture—you will understand a nation's pride.

OVERVIEW

The National Mall is a one-and-a-half-mile rectangular memorial park. It is home to world-famous historical monuments, memorials, sculptures, and statues of presidents and influential leaders—sometimes heartwarmingly called America's backyard. There are art galleries honoring fallen soldiers from prominent wars and significant political figures. It's a multiple museum paradise of which many are Smithsonian (meaning free entry) with reflecting pools to enhance their impressiveness. The cherry blossoms in bloom during the early Summer season at the tidal base area are most still the offspring of the original tree saplings, which were a gift from Japan in 1912. The Mall receives about 32 million annual international visitors. There are about 55 sites of interest to visit, which include the four main icons (including the White House and its

Visitor's Center, the Washington Monument, Lincoln Memorial, and the Capitol Building), 24 Museums, 14 Memorials, and about 11 other diverse attractions (including the U.S. Botanical Gardens).

The National Mall is at the heartbeat of downtown Washington D.C. It can be reached via metro, public bus transportation, or private vehicle. The closest airports are Ronald Reagan Washington National Airport, Washington Dulles International Airport, and Baltimore/Washington International Thurgood Marshall Airport, and all have transportation services available that connect to the Mall. The following roads take you directly to the Mall (parking may be challenging):

- Interstate 395 connects from the South.
- From the West: Interstate 66 and U.S. Routes 29 and 50.
- From the North: Interstate 495, New York Avenue, Rock Creek, Potomac Parkway, Cabin John Parkway, and George Washington Memorial Parkway.
- U.S. Routes 1, 4, and 50 take you from the East.
- The area covers a vast federal landscape from the U.S. Capitol moving West toward the Potomac River and Lincoln Memorial. The Washington Monument is centered slightly West of the midpoint of the National Mall. If you struggle to find the area, simply follow the iconic obelisk-shaped Washington Monument, which used to be one of the tallest places on earth before the Eiffel Tower stole its shine!

The most rewarding hours to visit the Mall (open 24 hours a day) are when the sun plays with the start of the day or in the early evening when many reflections enhance your internal reflection before the lights spark another emotional ambiance. A basic tour of the area should take you a minimum of five hours, from which you can regulate specific sites to re-visit. Apart from some of the most iconic architectural, historical buildings, the area provides a beautiful display of 1,000 acres of parks, promenades, and reflective water features to enhance relaxation as you wander through them. A visit to the park will be an educational journey of the symbols of the nation's democratic values to evoke pride and nationalism, enhance respect for civilian sacrifices or contributions, and honor distinguished people and events' legacies.

THE GUIDED TOURS

There are about seven to nine miles to be covered, so a good option is to take a bicycle and avoid parking issues. An even better suggestion is to take a guided tour that will focus on the best options instead of spending the day just walking aimlessly around. Or you can download the National Mall app to guide your itinerary and planning.

The Types of Tours

Let's have a look at some transportation and tour options available. More information can be found online.

Big Bus Tours

Open-top sightseeing bus tours are very popular and informative, and they offer a 24 or 48-hour hop-on/hop-off option to see most of the iconic landmarks of the Mall. This is a very entertaining way to explore the seriousness of the memorials, and buses take you up close to the sites for detailed exploration. The area also has National Park Rangers stationed in the area to assist with any questions.

Tours of the National Buildings

- The Capital Building: These tours should be made well in advance on the visitthecapitol.gov website. From the Capitol Visitor Center, a guided tour starts with a short introduction film and visits to the Crypt, Rotunda, and National Statuary Hall. US residents can also arrange tours through their state Senator. These tours can be more personalized and allow you access to areas the other tours don't go to. You will go through security screening so it is recommended that you carry as few items as possible.

- The White House: Tours must be scheduled well in advance through local state Congress members for U.S. residents, and foreigners must make arrangements through their local embassy in Washington, D.C. Upon arrival, you will be required to go through security as well as all those over 18 years of age showing ID (either a passport or USA driver's license or government issued ID.) Make sure you arrive on time and follow the procedures as outlined in your confirmation. Limit items you have with you, including backpacks, water bottles, and other items. Cell phones and small cameras are allowed, but no videos or flash photos are permitted. Tours are free and self-guided. Note that your tour may be canceled at the last minute based on events happening inside the White House that day.

- Supreme Court Building - Self-guided tours of the Supreme Court are also available when the court is not in session. Hours are typically 9 AM to 4:30 PM, Monday – Friday. You will need to be quiet as the working areas are near the public areas. No photos or videos are allowed in the courtroom.

- The Bureau of Engraving and Printing – at the time of publication, tours are not allowed. If you wish to visit, check https://www.bep.gov/visitor-centers before your visit to see if this has changed.

- The National Archives – No appointments are needed to enter here. However, they only allow a limited number of people in at a time, and the line can get very long. It is recommended that you arrive up to 30 minutes before opening for the best experience. This is where you will see an original copy of the Bill of Rights, Constitution, and other national documents.

Private Tours:

Luxurious private tours, customized tours, walking tours (day and night), bicycle tours, and many more offer options for discovering the sites effectively. A multitude of tour guides is available online to suit your specific needs. Although some attractions require pre-booking and payment, like the Washington Monument, the following memorials need no reservations:

- Lincoln Memorial
- Jefferson Memorial
- National World War II Memorial
- Martin Luther King, Jr. Memorial
- Vietnam Veterans Memorial
- FDR Memorial

The Tricycle Tours

Adventure DC Tricycle Tours offers customized day or night tours of the National Mall monuments and memorials, including free pick-up/drop-off services. They are pet-friendly, child-friendly, and mobility-impaired-friendly. In addition to all of this, they also guide the tour with a very entertaining narration of the historical facts and stories behind the attractions while you are being transported in a shaded coach!

Segway Tours

The City Segway tours are probably the most unique option for a stress-free visit to the attractions. It takes a few minutes to get used to the feeling, to balance, and manipulate the movement when you take a segway for the first time. After this, it is simply a lot of fun. You have to be 16 years old (weight limits apply as well as a healthy sense of balance!) to take these tours. Their biggest advantage is that you get to see so much more with the least difficulty. Group tours can be arranged on these nimble sets of wheels. There are many options available, and most of them last about two and a half hours. They include all your safety gear, provide wireless audio headsets, and cost around $65 for tours that can be arranged daily—offering daytime, sunset, or specialized night tour options. Some tours take you to about 25 notable sites, and others offer only an overview of fewer attractions. Groups can vary between 8–12 people, depending on the operator.

THE TOP THINGS TO DO IN THE NATIONAL MALL

There are too many things to do at the Mall. The following are items that should top your list of activities while visiting Washington, D.C.

For All

Smithsonian National Museum of Natural History

This is the second most visited Natural History Museum in the world. There are collections of more than 145 million specimens of animals, fossils, plants, minerals, rocks (including the stunning Hope Diamond), human remains, and cultural artifacts, which is the most comprehensive natural history collection in the world. It also houses the "largest group of scientists dedicated to the study of natural and cultural history in the world" (Wikipedia Contributors, 2019a). The museum aims to give an appreciation of the natural world and our sensitive cultural interaction with the planet. The museum is on 1oth Street and Constitution Avenue, Washington D.C., and visitors can also enter from Madison Drive. It's open 364 days of the year (closed on Christmas Day) from 10 a.m. to 5:30 p.m., and entry is free. The collections are a true record of human interaction with its environment and thus tell the story of our planet's natural development and history. The vital role that we play in the sustainability of our planet is at the core of their mission. Many programs, exhibitions (geology, human origins, fossil hall, hall of mammals, ocean hall, African voices exhibit, insect zoo, hall of bones), webinars, and regular auditorium events focus on informative interaction with the public.

The Butterfly Pavilion (a ticketed venue at a small fee—except for free Tuesdays) inside the museum is the most popular venue where you can walk among the fluttering butterflies and tropical plants. Sometimes they even land on you for a quick rest! Also, the rare giant squid exhibit in the ocean hall is a definite wow factor for the kids. They will love the discovery room and its interactive displays to touch. Oh, and letting some insects walk on their hands... There are some dining and shopping facilities. If you cannot make it to The National Museum of American History, a visit to this museum will keep young minds occupied.

(An interesting fact: the museum and some of its exhibitions are featured in a couple of famous movies and video games—*Get Smart, The Dagger of Amon Ra, Fallout 3,* and *Night at the Museum: Battle of the Smithsonian*.)

The Lincoln Memorial

This magnificent 27,336-square foot memorial was built between 1914 and 1922 in the Neoclassical temple style and has been a famous site for many important speeches—including the freedom speech made by Martin Luther King, Jr. in 1963. To go and linger in the breath of history and memory at this site is a vacation in itself. The imposing memorial (and its exquisite reflection in twilight hours) is situated on the far west end of the National Mall and looks toward the Washington Monument and Capitol building. GPS coordinates are 38°53'21.4" N and 77°3'0.5" W. You can gain direct access from Constitution Avenue and 23rd Street.

Not many words can describe the inner experience of being at the memorial. It is a place that every person has to see for themselves—to feel the emotions well up as you climb the stairs and see the huge marble statue of solitary contemplation. President Lincoln watches the skies change color as the evening skies produce a magnificent reflection of the memorial in the reflecting pool just outside. The epitaph above his tranquil gaze holds the moment beautifully, "In this temple as in the hearts of the people for whom he saved the Union, the memory of Abraham Lincoln is enshrined forever" (Wikipedia Contributors, 2018) as it echoes the symbolism of strength, wisdom, and unity. Goosebump material moments!

The Air and Space Museum

Calling all future astronauts and pilots to the impressive air and space artifacts that you will not easily see at any other museum! The Air and Space Museum at the National Mall showcases the incredible technological advances made over the past century in aerial exploration. It is child-friendly, with a gallery that is designed purely for them. No wonder it is one of the most popular museums in the world. The main entrance is at 600 Independence Avenue, between the 4th and 7th Streets intersections, Washington D.C. and the back of the building faces Jefferson Drive. Timed-entry passes have to be reserved online to gain entry, even though they are free of charge. Individual passes and group passes are available.

A multitude of educational programs, regularly updated events, science demonstrations, interactive discovery stations, and extraordinary aeronautical exhibitions will make jaws drop and necks hurt from looking up all the time. Make time to take the kids to the story time reading, where they can hear fantastic tales for inspiration about trips to other planets, hot-air balloonists, world-famous aviators and aviatrixes, and winged inventions, to name a few. After the experience, the kids can take home the craft activity that they make at the venue. The museum is currently undergoing huge transformations, and in October 2022, eight new galleries will open to the public. The museum plans to open more in the next three years after extensive renovations. These reimaginings and upgrades may affect opening times (the IMAX theater, some tours, educational programs, the Observatory, and some galleries may also be closed to the public during the upgrade process).

The Washington Monument

The tallest structure in D.C., made of marble, bluestone gneiss, and granite, dominates the skyline with its obelisk frame. It took

36 years to complete, and the shade of stone color differences is quite obvious. As the memorial for the first president of the US, the monument has witnessed the shaping of the country's history like no other, and it pays tribute to George Washington's leadership and contributions. Although plans for a national monument started in 1783 already, the final memorial was only opened to the public more than a hundred years later (in 1888) after lots of political turmoil and financial setbacks. It's impossible to miss the site, right at the center of the Mall between Constitution and Independence Avenues.

It doesn't really matter what time of the day you go to view this unique attraction; the experience will be different every time as the landscape and light play along. Sometimes it reflects on the water, and in the twilight hours, the colors of the sky enhance its magnificence. Inside you will have some of the most breathtaking views for about 40 miles from the top of the 555 feet monument. Tours are available and can be booked in advance online. All visitors need entry tickets from the age of two years up. These free tickets can be obtained on the day on site from 8:45 a.m. but make sure to arrive early as the queues can become quite long (especially during peak season), and tickets are limited. A limited number of 24-hour or 30-day reservations can be made online for a nominal fee at 10 a.m. but make sure to get them as soon as online portals open before they are also sold out.

The Spy Museum

Do your little ones have a keen espionage interest? Then they will excel in the interactive fun of the Spy Museum, where present-day investigations and past spy life and culture are exhibited. You will be assigned a mission and can either do your own mission or share it as a family as you explore the museum. They even have an entire display dedicated to James Bond and his shenanigans. The Museum is within walking distance from the Wharf at L'Enfant Plaza in Southwest D.C. There is a fee to get into the museum and it is recommended that you purchase your tickets online. Even with scheduled arrival times, the museum can get crowded during peak times. If you can't visit during a non-peak time of year, I recommend scheduling as early in the morning as you can to avoid the heavier crowds of the day.

The National Zoo (Pandas)

The Smithsonian National Zoo (at 3001 Connecticut Avenue) is 163 acres of learning stations and animal shelters with landscaped lawn areas. Here the kids will meet all their wildlife friends again and also some that they have never seen before! There are more than 2000 animals, including red pandas, elephants, buffalo, flamingos, aquatic animals, reptiles, arachnids, and even cows and catfish. The National Zoo is 1 of only 4 zoos in the USA where you can see giant pandas on loan from China. The most popular fun event is the *Snore and Roar* overnight (and very informative) camping adventure in a tent while listening to the sounds of wild animals and learning more about them. This old Zoo was founded in 1889 already! See The National Zoo website for more information on the pandas and various programs.

Dinner Cruises

Experience the beauty of the Mall from the Potomac River on a luxury climate-controlled cruise boat that offers premier three-course dining experiences ranging from a stylish brunch or lunch to a glamorous dinner buffet. The cruise boats depart from Pier 4 at 580 Water Street SW. The boats are within walking distance from the Waterfront Metro (two blocks away), and using public transport to get there is advisable because of parking challenges.

Boarding for brunch starts at 10:45 a.m. and departs at 11:30 a.m. Lunch cruises board at 11:15 a.m. for a noon departure. Boarding for the Signature Dinner Cruise starts at 6 p.m., and the cruise starts an hour later and ends at 10 p.m. (On Sundays, the schedules are shorter and start at 5 p.m.) Dress is smart casual cocktail attire, and reservations are important. It's a slightly longer than two-hour cruise that includes onboard entertainment, DJ or live music, and dancing at night. The dining cruise prices at the time of publication range from $60–$120 per person, depending on the time of the day. Kids have reduced prices, under three years old join for free. This is an unforgettable family experience and should not be missed!

For Teens

Smithsonian Castle

Of all the museums that you plan to visit in D.C., the Smithsonian Castle (the National Mall's iconic red building) is probably the first and most prominent one to see. The history of the man who founded all the Smithsonian museums is a fascinating tale in itself. James Smithson, 1765–1829, was the illegitimate son (French-born but raised in the UK) of a Duke. He became a British Scientist. He—

left his considerable fortune to a nephew with the stipulation that, were the nephew to die without heirs, the money goes 'to the United States of America, to found at Washington, under the name of the Smithsonian Institution, an establishment for the increase and diffusion of knowledge.' The nephew died, and a museum complex was born (Washington.org, 2016).

Ironically, he never set foot in America, and he died in Italy, but his legacy and profound bequest remain a mystery to the world. The first Smithsonian building (this distinctive red sandstone castle) opened to the public in 1855, and even today, the neo-Gothic structure has matured with the times. It hosts contemporary displays, curious exhibits, maps information, and offers small displays about other Smithsonian museums. The building is home to the visitor's center as well. It also holds his marble crypt in a chapel-like room—probably the most treasured aspect of the distinctive building. This venue is situated between 7th and 12th Streets on Jefferson Drive, and it is a sure attention grabber with its brilliant red facade.

Tidal Basin

The tidal basin is 107 acres, 10 feet average depth, artificial tidal pool with primary inflows from the Potomac River. During the spectacular Spring cherry blossoms season and festival, when this reservoir becomes the focal point, nothing is better than a paddle cruise on the Tidal Basin. This can be done any time of the year up to the Jefferson Memorial. It has two functions, namely, to flush the Washington Channel and also as a visual centerpiece of beauty. Boats can be rented opposite the Jefferson Memorial at the dock on most days of the year. GPS coordinates are 38°53'03" N and 77°02'21" W, Washington D.C. From the boats, you can see many of the memorials and also the iconic Washington Monument. (Significant holidays boats rental are excluded)

Sunset and Kayak Tour (The Potomac River)

A wide selection of tours and boat rentals are available to enjoy the Potomac River scenery. One such experience is a kayak tour at sunset. This is a very appropriate option for young kids since kayaks can be managed by any child over 8 years. Not much skill is required for a kayak trip, and it is an easy way to paddle the water for beginners. A 90-minute kayak sunset tour is available at *Boating in DC*, starting from Key Bridge Boathouse. They also offer lessons and guidance by experienced instructors and apply a high level of safety measures. These tours promise to generate a completely different and new perspective of the city. It combines the historic memorial experience with activity in a natural landscape. Season passes are available from a large selection of tour operators to enhance the relaxing experience even more.

For Kids

The Botanic Gardens

The United States Botanic Gardens (USBG) is one of the oldest botanic gardens in North America since its establishment in

1820. It is a good option for slightly chilly days. This living plant museum has a large indoor conservatory and outdoor gardens. The historic greenhouse consists of two courtyard gardens and ten glassed garden rooms of nearly 29,000 square feet. The children's garden is closed during Winter. USBG receives more than a million visitors per year. Four blocks from the Federal Center metro station, metro buses (32, 34, and 36) take visitors directly to the conservatory located on Independence and First Street. The main entrance is at 100 Maryland Avenue. It's open daily from 10 a.m. to 5 p.m., and the gated outdoor gardens for longer hours (365 days of the year) offer free entry.

With the aim to encourage sustainable gardening, it informs visitors of the fundamental importance and value of plant diversity, as well as their aesthetic, ecological, economic, cultural, and therapeutic importance. There is a multitude of exhibits, tours, workshops, regular programs, even cooking demonstrations, and an annual popular holiday show adding a festive touch with its large display of poinsettias, plant material models of the DC monuments, and a "fantasy train display."

There is simply too much to see to mention!

Smithsonian Carousel

A whimsical touch to the otherwise rather serious National Mall with an interesting bit of history is the beautiful carousel. The one exceptional element about the carousel (after it was built in the 1940s) was its technical achievement. It was the only carousel with four jumping horses abreast at the time, but the real controversial issue was the racial barring of non-white participants. It took a decade of protests to change the law and desegregation the ride. On August 28, 1963, the 11-month-old Sharon Langley became the first Black child who rode the merry-go-round along with White children and her parents, signifying freedom as the carousel went around.

The carousel is right in the middle of the Mall, in front of the Smithsonian Arts and Industries building, numbers 867–919 Jefferson Drive. It has easy access from the Smithsonian metro station and is open from 10 a.m. to 6 p.m. (and until 5 p.m. in Winter). Sometimes, there are even puppet shows and musical entertainment in the area. The first carousel was installed in 1967 and then upgraded to a new one in 1981. It's still open most days of the year, and at the time of publication, kids can enjoy the ride for a mere $3,50!

Takeaways

- Bring enough water, especially if you plan to visit during the warmer months.
- Have a large breakfast before venturing out; dining options are limited.
- Always wear comfortable walking shoes—there is lots of walking to be done.
- Dress appropriately for the activities that you plan to engage in.
- Prepare for the heat...

- Plan the visit!

There you have it! Some of the most popular destinations are perfect to start your epic family vacation. North America has so many unforgettable places to show the children, and none of these journeys should ever be missed. Hopefully, these few ones tickled your traveling ideas enough to start more.

CONCLUSION

A handful of the most unique bucket list experiences in the USA to share with your kids!

For unique family vacations, consider the following:

- The undeniable importance of engaging a qualified travel agent.
- The importance of de-stressing as a family unit from daily routines and challenges.
- Meticulous planning and preparation to make the vacation memorable but also stress-free.
- Keeping tips and advice in mind when traveling with kids.

For epic places to create vacation memories that the family can relive:

- The Grand Canyon in Arizona amazes with its grandeur and the remote landscapes of Havasupai. Sunset views will linger long after the days have gone.
- Nevada's Las Vegas glitter will shine in the children's smiles after the thrills of SkyPod and AdventureDome. Cirque du Soleil and its talented acrobats may just inspire some out-of-the-box thinking in curious young minds.

- Slowing down in Tennessee with the penguins, mountains and trees, and unique Craftsmen's Fair will enhance renewed relaxation.

- Experiences of the mysterious bubbling and gurgling of the earth at Yellowstone in Wyoming will be talked about for days on end.

- Historical sites and a treasure trove full of museums of all kinds at the National Mall in Washington D.C. is the best edu-vacation experience any child can wish for.

All that remains now is to focus on the incredible experience after a well-planned vacation, get ready to visit all the new places and create much-needed family time with this easy-to-plan guide that makes it easier for you.

If you found this book useful, do leave a review and tell me how it helped your planning and itinerary for the best family vacation ever!

Passing the Adventure Torch

Wow, you've made it to the end of our exciting journey together! Now that you and your family are superstars at planning amazing trips, it's time to share your newfound adventure secrets with the world.

Leaving your thoughts about "The Extraordinary Family Travel Guide, Bucket List USA" on Amazon is like passing a magical torch. Your review will guide other families who are just starting their journey and looking for the best travel tips and coolest destinations.

By sharing your honest opinion, you'll show other adventurous families where they can find the same awesome advice and exciting ideas that helped you. Think of it as your way of keeping the spirit of family adventures alive and sparkling!

Thank you for being such an important part of this journey. Every time we share our travel stories and tips, we keep the excitement and wonder of exploring new places alive. And you're helping do just that!

✸>>> Click here or scan the QR Code to blaze a trail with your review on Amazon.<<<✸

https://www.amazon.com/review/review-your-purchases/?asin=1960049003

Remember, every review is like a shining star in the travel universe, guiding other families to amazing experiences. You're not just leaving a review; you're lighting the way for others to create unforgettable memories, just like you did.

Keep exploring, keep sharing, and keep the adventure alive!

Your travel guide and fellow explorer,

Jacklene Conner

REFERENCES

Absolon, M. (2020, November 30). Grand Canyon bicycle FAQ. Grand Canyon National Park Trips. https://www.mygrandcanyonpark.com/things-to-do/biking/by-bicycle/

Adventure DC Tricycle Tours. (n.d.). *Adventure DC tricycle tours.* Adventuredctricyclestours.com. https://adventure-dc-tricycle-tours.business.site/

AllTrips.com. (2022). *Yellowstone horseback riding, horse trail rides.* AllTrips - Yellowstone National Park. https://www.yellowstoneparknet.com/summer_recreation/horseback_riding.php

Anakeesta TM. (2022a). *About Anakeesta - A magical theme park in the mountains!* Anakeesta. https://anakeesta.com/about/

Anakeesta TM. (2022b). Anakeesta theme park in the mountains of Gatlinburg Tennessee. Anakeesta. https://anakeesta.com/

Arcadia. (2022). *Home.* Arcadia. https://gatlinburgarcade.com/

Arciniega, C. (2022). *8 best segway tours in Washington DC (2022) | free tours by foot.* Https://Freetoursbyfoot.com/. https://freetoursbyfoot.com/segway-tours-washington-dc/

Ascen. (2020, July 15). *Best Grand Canyon helicopter tour of 2020 and my experience.* Capture the Atlas. https://capturetheatlas.com/grand-canyon-helicopter-tour/

Booth, J. (2019, February 2). *The Grand Canyon is one of the 7 natural wonders of the world. Here are 13 things you might not know about it.* Insider. https://www.insider.com/things-you-didnt-know-about-the-grand-canyon-2019-2#the-grand-canyon-museum-has-reportedly-exposed-tourists-to-uranium-for-18-years-13

Breakout. (2022). *#1 escape room in Gatlinburg | breakout Games® official site.* Breakout. https://breakoutgames.com/gatlinburg

BRGSM. (2016). *Arcadia Gatlinburg.* Smoky Mountains Brochures. https://smokymountainsbrochures.com/coupons/arcadia-family-fun-arcade-gatlinburg/

Bright Angel Bicycles. (2016). *Bike Grand Canyon.* Bike Grand Canyon. https://bikegrandcanyon.com/

Brownson, J. (2018, May 29). *33 best tips for amazing family travel with your kids (less stress & more fun!).* UpgradedPoints.com. https://upgradedpoints.com/travel/best-tips-family-travel-with-kids/

Camp TravelExplore. (2021, August 6). *20 stops in 4 days at Yellowstone national park | things to do in Yellowstone national park.* 20 STOPS in 4 DAYS at YELLOWSTONE NATIONAL PARK | Things to Do in Yellowstone National Park. https://youtu.be/yHgBH9uhPCg

Carathers, A. (2022, September 6). *15 Gatlinburg fall foliage spots | downtown, drives & trails.* Www.gatlinburg.com. https://www.gatlinburg.com/blog/post/15-best-places-to-see-the-fall-colors-in-gatlinburg-and-the-great-smoky-mountains-national-park/

CareerExplorer. (2017, July 11). *What does a travel agent do?* Careerexplorer.com; CareerExplorer. https://www.careerexplorer.com/careers/travel-agent/

Circus Circus Las Vegas. (n.d.). *Adventuredome tickets*. Etrac.ticketcostars.com. https://etrac.ticketcostars.com/portal/adventuredome.html

Circus Circus Las Vegas. (2022). *The adventuredome at Circus Circus Las Vegas | Circus Circus hotel & casino Las Vegas*. Circus Circus | Circus Circus Hotel & Casino Las Vegas. https://www.circuscircus.com/the-adventuredome/rides-attractions-1/

Cirque du Soleil. (n.d.-a). *Best of teeterboard | cirque du soleil*. Www.youtube.com. https://youtu.be/vPEYDfIj9Kg

Cirque du Soleil. (n.d.-b). Whisk you away to Las Vegas! | 60-minute special #13 | cirque du soleil | mystère, o, kà. Www.youtube.com. https://youtu.be/EVY1-nH-fVU

Cirque du Soleil. (2012, June 28). *KÀ from Cirque du Soleil - official preview*. Www.youtube.com. https://youtu.be/Pmqz_gdiY8o

Cirque du Soleil. (2015, October 16). *The theatre of KÀ by Cirque du Soleil | KÀ: Behind the blockbuster*. Www.youtube.com. https://youtu.be/csS2N5YDtu4

Cirque du Soleil. (2021, February 26). *Spotlight on: crystal | cirque du soleil*. Www.youtube.com. https://youtu.be/1u9NANaHutg

CirqueConnect. (n.d.). *Your access to cirque du soleil content, all in one place*. Cirqueconnect.cirquedusoleil.com. https://cirqueconnect.cirquedusoleil.com/?shows=mystere

City Experiences anchored by Hornblower. (2022). *Premier dinner cruise | city cruises*. City Experiences Anchored by Hornblower. https://www.cityexperiences.com/washington-dc/city-cruises/hornblower-odyssey-dinner-cruise/

Clark, J. (2017, August 3). *Yellowstone: A perfect morning for wildlife watching*. Yellowstone National Park Lodges. https://www.yellowstonenationalparklodges.com/connect/yellowstone-hot-spot/yellowstone-a-perfect-morning-for-wildlife-watching/

Clark, J. (2018, August 2). *Yellowstone: Where the bison roam*. Yellowstone National Park Lodges. https://www.yellowstonenationalparklodges.com/connect/yellowstone-hot-spot/yellowstone-where-the-bison-roam/

Cross, B. (2022). *Arcade city - play - the island in Pigeon Forge, TN*. The Island in Pigeon Forge. https://islandinpigeonforge.com/poi/arcade-city/

Cuddy, R. (2020, May 1). *25 awesome and fun things to do in DC for teens*. DC Travel Magazine. https://dctravelmag.com/things-to-do-in-dc-for-teens/

Dan at More Old Stuff. (2016, March 17). *Sky jump Las Vegas stratosphere- we did it!* Www.youtube.com. https://youtu.be/KgLrnyh5FYc

Dana. (2013, February 25). *The Smithsonian carousel - Washington, DC*. Calgaryplaygroundreview.com. https://calgaryplaygroundreview.com/the-smithsonian-carousel-washington-dc/

Dana, & Calgary Playground Review. (2013, November 30). *Visiting the national mall with kids - Washington, DC*.

Calgaryplaygroundreview.com. https://calgaryplaygroundreview.com/visiting-national-mall-kids-washington-dc/

Dollywood. (2020). *Dollywood*. Dollywood.com. https://www.dollywood.com/

East Yellowstone Lodging. (2022). *East Yellowstone lodging | lodging near Yellowstone east entrance cody*. East Yellowstone Lodging. https://yellowstone-lodging.com/?utm_source=AllTrips&utm_campaign=AllTrips-AllYellowstonePark.com&utm_medium=referral&utm_content=/summer_recreation/horseback_riding

Exploration To Go. (2021, December 20). *Exploring Treasure Island in Las Vegas, Nevada USA walking tour*. Www.youtube.com. https://youtu.be/n-QuF6JG01I

Face Amusement Group. (2019). *Arcade city*. FACE. https://faceamusement.com/arcade-city/

Fine Tip Creative Studio. (2022, April 29). *Avengers Station Las Vegas | video tour*. Www.youtube.com. https://youtu.be/RLw1rKEGLD8

finleyholiday. (2020, June 17). *Bryce, Zion & the north rim of the grand canyon*. Www.youtube.com. https://youtu.be/dVYnB-tKrfk

Future Unity. (2022, August 4). *New discovery at Yellowstone national park that scared scientists!* Www.youtube.com. https://youtu.be/2CCG-UtTKuc

Gallivanter, C. (2021a, December 21). *10 things you must do in Gatlinburg, Tennessee*. Www.youtube.com. https://youtu.be/18w73UB9HzM

Gallivanter, C. (2021b, December 27). *10 things you must do in Pigeon Forge, Tennessee*. Www.youtube.com. https://youtu.be/OKEDm6zzpNM

Gatlinburg Craftsmen's Fair. (n.d.). *Gatlinburg craftsmen's fair*. Www.facebook.com. https://www.facebook.com/gatlinburgcraftsmensfair/

Gatlinburg Craftsmen's Fair. (2017a). *Gatlinburg craftsmen's fair home*. Gatlinburg Craftsmens Fair. https://craftsmenfair.com/

Gatlinburg Craftsmen's Fair. (2017b). *Gatlinburg craftsmen's fair july 2021 | shop handmade art & crafts*. Gatlinburg Craftsmens Fair. https://craftsmenfair.com/july-fair/

Gatlinburg Mountain Coaster. (2015, April 2). Ride the Gatlinburg mountain coaster - the most exhilarating thrill ride in the Smoky Mountains! Www.youtube.com. https://youtu.be/00AwX8lnmK8

Gatlinburg Skylift. (2022a). *Best Smoky Mountain views and lift ride | Gatlinburg skylift & skybridge, Tennessee*. Www.gatlinburgskylift.com. https://www.gatlinburgskylift.com/

Gatlinburg Skylift. (2022b). *Gatlinburg skylift park tickets*. Www.gatlinburgskylift.com. https://www.gatlinburgskylift.com/tickets

Gatlinburg TN. (2016). *Gatlinburg, TN | the smoky mountains are calling*. Gatlinburg, TN. https://www.gatlinburg.com/

Gatlinburg TN. (2019). *Welcome to Gatlinburg, tn*. Gatlinburgtn.gov. https://www.gatlinburgtn.gov/

Gatlinburg TN. (2021). *Welcome to Gatlinburg, tn.* Www.gatlinburgtn.gov. https://www.gatlinburgtn.gov/news_detail_T6_R265.php

gatlinburgskylift. (2019, August 26). *Gatlinburg skybridge: Behind the scenes.* Www.youtube.com. https://youtu.be/x7mlgq9t-vw

Geli, N. (2022, March 5). *What not to do in Las Vegas.* Www.youtube.com. https://youtu.be/naiwnqzjqys

Grand Canyon National Park Trips. (n.d.). *Biking archives.* Grand Canyon National Park Trips. https://www.mygrandcanyonpark.com/things-to-do/biking/

Grand Canyon National Park Trips. (2020, July 23). *10 best things to do with kids in the Grand Canyon.* Grand Canyon National Park Trips. https://www.mygrandcanyonpark.com/things-to-do/park-itineraries/kids-activities-grand-canyon/

Grand Canyon Youth. (2018, August 1). *Individual expeditions * Grand Canyon youth.* Grand Canyon Youth. https://gcyouth.org/expeditions/individual-expeditions/

Guest Services. (2022). *Boating in DC kayaking, paddling, passes, tours, classes.* Boating in DC. https://boatingindc.com/

Gwadzinski. (2019, December 2). *Yellowstone junior ranger programs for kids.* Yellowstone National Park. https://www.yellowstonepark.com/things-to-do/park-itineraries/kids-programs-activities/

Hamilton, T. (n.d.). *Adventuredome theme park Circus Circus - hours, ticket discounts.* Vegas Unzipped. https://www.vegasunzipped.com/adventuredome-theme-park/

Hamper, A. (2020, February 7). *Tennessee in pictures: 15 beautiful places to photograph | planetware*. Www.planetware.com. https://www.planetware.com/pictures/tennessee-ustn.htm

Havasupai Tribe. (2017). *Havasupai lodge*. Theofficialhavasupaitribe.com. https://theofficialhavasupaitribe.com/Havasupai-Lodge/havasupai-lodge.html

Hayden valley | introduction to Yellowstone. (2017). Yellowstone.net. https://yellowstone.net/intro/hayden-valley/

History.com Editors. (2018, August 21). *Grand Canyon*. HISTORY. https://www.history.com/topics/landmarks/grand-canyon

Hooper, M. (2022, August 7). *Adventuredome: Rides, Prices & Hours In August 2022*. Vegasfoodandfun.com. https://vegasfoodandfun.com/adventuredome/

Hotels.com. (2013). Treasure Island in Las Vegas - experience a world-class resort escape at the centre of the Vegas strip - go guides. Hotels.com. https://uk.hotels.com/go/usa/treasure-island-las-vegas?pos=HCOM_UK&locale=en_GB

Hotels.com. (2022). *The adventuredome in Las Vegas - an indoor park with endless adventures - go guides*. Hotels.com. https://uk.hotels.com/go/usa/the-adventuredome-las-vegas?pos=HCOM_UK&locale=en_GB

https://plus.google.com/u/0/115914292287376697079?rel=author. (2016, March 23). *Pigeon Forge or Gatlinburg â€" where should I stay?* Cabins USA Pigeon Forge Cabins in the Smoky Mountains. https://www.cabinsusa.com/smoky-mountains-blog/post/203/pigeon-forge-vs-gatlinburg--which-is-better.php

https://www.facebook.com/fullsuitcase. (2019, February 7). *16 absolute best things to do in Yellowstone*. Full Suitcase Family Travel Blog - Trips with Kids and Travel Tips. https://fullsuitcase.com/yellowstone-best-things-to-do/

IMEG. (2021, March 16). *Top 7 mountain coasters in Gatlinburg and Pigeon Forge*. Visit My Smokies. https://www.visitmysmokies.com/blog/attractions-gatlinburg/mountain-coasters-gatlinburg-pigeon-forge/

In and Out of Vegas. (2022, June 17). *Marvel Avengers STATION | Treasure Island Las Vegas*. Www.youtube.com. https://youtu.be/fEhjlRDObko

Jackson-Cannady, A. (2019, May 30). *12 cool things to do with kids at the national mall*. Tinybeans. https://tinybeans.com/dc/national-mall-washington-dc-with-kids/slide/1

Jurga. (2018, June 29). *Boiling River in Yellowstone national park (complete guide)*. Full Suitcase Family Travel Blog. https://fullsuitcase.com/boiling-River-yellowstone/

Jurga. (2019, February 7). *16 absolute best things to do in Yellowstone*. Full Suitcase Family Travel Blog - Trips with Kids and Travel Tips. https://fullsuitcase.com/yellowstone-best-things-to-do/

Jurga. (2020a, January 27). *Best time to visit Yellowstone (+ tips for each season)*. Full Suitcase Family Travel Blog. https://fullsuitcase.com/best-time-to-visit-yellowstone/

Jurga. (2020b, May 30). *11 best Yellowstone tours & guided excursions for 2022 (+ info & tips)*. Full Suitcase Family Travel Blog. https://fullsuitcase.com/yellowstone-tours/

kidcentral tn. (n.d.). *Vacations have a positive impact on the entire family!* Www.kidcentraltn.com. https://www.kidcentraltn.com/support/full-family-support/vacations-have-a-positive-impact-on-the-entire-family--.html#:~:text=Family%2520vacations%2520not%2520only%2520build

Kollar, L. (2017, November 2). *13 reasons why you should visit Tennessee*. Culture Trip. https://theculturetrip.com/north-america/usa/tennessee/articles/13-reasons-why-you-should-visit-tennessee/

Kwak-Hefferan, E. (2021, April 13). *About old faithful, Yellowstone's famous geyser*. Yellowstone National Park. https://www.yellowstonepark.com/things-to-do/geysers-hot-springs/about-old-faithful/

Kwak-Hefferan, E. (2022, May 6). *Watch wildlife in lamar valley and hayden valley*. Yellowstone National Park. https://www.yellowstonepark.com/things-to-do/wildlife/lamar-hayden-valley/

Lanin, C. (2020, March 3). *Grand Canyon with kids: 17 activities for families*. TravelMamas.com. https://travelmamas.com/grand-canyon-with-kids/

LasVegasHowTo. (2022). *The adventuredome theme park*. Lasvegashowto.com. https://www.lasvegashowto.com/adventuredome

lasvegaskids.net. (2022). *12 ways to get free or discounted adventuredome tickets - coupons, prices, groupon*. Www.lasvegaskids.net. https://www.lasvegaskids.net/things-to-do/adventuredome-coupons/

Marcoux, H. (2021, June 16). *Vacations make your kids happy after they're over - motherly.* Www.mother.ly. https://www.mother.ly/health-wellness/its-science/want-to-make-your-family-happier-go-on-vacation-says-study/

Mastercard. (n.d.). *89 percent of Americans are stressed out over planning family vacations.* MasterCard Social Newsroom. https://newsroom.mastercard.com/press-releases/89-percent-of-americans-are-stressed-out-over-planning-family-vacations/

Mastercard News. (n.d.). *All sizes | INFOGRAPHIC: Vacations are stressing families out | flickr - photo sharing!* Www.flickr.com. https://www.flickr.com/photos/mastercardnews/14243225863/sizes/h/

Midway Mayhem. (2019, December 12). *Zamperla nebulaz spinning ride POV IAAPA 2019.* https://www.youtube.com/watch?v=4O79cuy2fLE

Minnaert, Dr. L. (2019). *Family travel association dr. Lynn Minnaert.* https://www.sps.nyu.edu/content/dam/sps/academics/departments/jonathan-m--tisch-center-for-hospitality/pdfs/Family_Travel_Survey_2019.pdf

Monga, P. (2021, December 7). *10 family travel tips for a hassle free vacation with your loved ones.* Travel Triangle. https://traveltriangle.com/blog/family-travel-tips/

Moonshine Mountain Coaster. (2022). *Moonshine mountain coaster in Gatlinburg, TN.* Moonshine Mountain Coaster | Gatlinburg, Tennessee. https://www.moonshinemountaincoaster.com/

National Geographic. (2017, April 22). *Spend a relaxing hour in Yellowstone's beautiful landscapes | National Geographic*. Www.youtube.com. https://youtu.be/1VyhG3ypG5s

National Geographic. (2020, December 7). *Yellowstone (full episode) | America's national parks*. Www.youtube.com. https://www.youtube.com/watch?v=7OMxBlK46wY&t=7s

National Park Foundation. (2022). *Washington monument*. National Park Foundation. https://www.nationalparks.org/explore/parks/washington-monument

National Park Lodges. (2017). *Old faithful inn | yellowstone national park lodges*. Yellowstone National Park Lodges. https://www.yellowstonenationalparklodges.com/lodgings/hotel/old-faithful-inn/

National Park Lodges. (2020). *Lake yellowstone hotel & cabins | yellowstone national park lodges*. Yellowstone National Park Lodges. https://www.yellowstonenationalparklodges.com/lodgings/cabin/lake-yellowstone-hotel-cabins/

National Park Service. (n.d.-a). *8 pm: Evening program — S. rim village ranger program (U.S. national park service)*. Www.nps.gov. https://www.nps.gov/thingstodo/8-pm-evening-program-s-rim-village-ranger-program.htm

National Park Service. (n.d.-b). *Desert view sunset talks — program topics (U.S. national park service)*. Www.nps.gov. https://www.nps.gov/thingstodo/desert-view-sunset-talks.htm

National Park Service. (n.d.-c). *Directions - national mall and memorial parks (U.S. national park service)*. Www.nps.gov. https://www.nps.gov/nama/planyourvisit/directions.htm

National Park Service. (n.d.-d). *Frequently asked questions - national mall and memorial parks (U.S. National Park Service)*. Www.nps.gov. https://www.nps.gov/nama/faqs.htm

National Park Service. (n.d.-e). *Norris geyser basin trails (U.S. National Park Service)*. Www.nps.gov. https://www.nps.gov/thingstodo/yell-norris-geyser-basin-trails.htm

National Park Service. (n.d.-f). *Park ranger programs - winter 2020 - Grand Canyon national park (U.S. national park service)*. Www.nps.gov. https://www.nps.gov/grca/planyourvisit/ranger-program.htm

National Park Service. (n.d.-g). *Plan your visit - national mall and memorial parks (U.S. National Park Service)*. Www.nps.gov. https://www.nps.gov/nama/planyourvisit/index.htm

National Park Service. (n.d.-h). *South rim village - ranger programs - Grand Canyon national park (U.S. national park service)*. Www.nps.gov. https://www.nps.gov/grca/planyourvisit/sr-programs.htm

National Park Service. (n.d.-i). *Swim and soak - Yellowstone national park (U.S. national park service)*. Www.nps.gov. https://www.nps.gov/yell/planyourvisit/swimming-soaking.htm

National Park Service. (2016a). *Yellowstone lake - Yellowstone national park (U.S. National Park Service)*. Nps.gov. https://www.nps.gov/yell/learn/nature/yellowstone-lake.htm

National Park Service. (2016b, December 31). *Lincoln memorial (U.S. national park service)*. Nps.gov. https://www.nps.gov/linc/index.htm

National Park Service. (2021, February 2). *Hydrothermal systems - Yellowstone national park (U.S. National Park Service)*. Www.nps.gov. https://www.nps.gov/yell/learn/nature/hydrothermal-systems.htm

National Park Service. (2022, July 26). *Desert view ranger programs - Grand Canyon national park (U.S. national park service)*. Www.nps.gov. https://www.nps.gov/grca/planyourvisit/dv-programs.htm

NeigborhoodScout. (2022). *Las Vegas, NV crime rates and statistics - neighborhoodscout*. Www.neighborhoodscout.com. https://www.neighborhoodscout.com/nv/las-vegas/crime#description

NextStop.TV. (2013, March 25). *Next stop: Washington DC - segway guided tour*. Www.youtube.com. https://youtu.be/t0bMHKPsPGo

Norris, R. R. (2022, March 30). *What is an edu-vacation, and why should your family should consider taking one?* Veranda. https://www.veranda.com/travel/a39566699/what-is-an-edu-vacation/

Our Whole Village. (2019, July 23). *Experiential family travel in Peru: A day in the Quechua village of Huilloc • our whole village*. Our Whole Village. https://ourwholevillage.com/experiential-family-travel-peru/

Our Whole Village. (2022, January 28). *10 reasons to use a family travel agent in 2022 • our whole village*. Our Whole Village.

https://ourwholevillage.com/10-reasons-to-use-a-family-travel-agent-in-2022/

Our Whole Village 2021. (2021). *Travel tips archives • our whole village %*. Our Whole Village. https://ourwholevillage.com/category/travel-tips/

Peek, L. (2018, October 4). *14 family vacation tips you need to know*. BabyQuip | Baby Gear Rentals & Cleaning. https://www.babyquip.com/blog/family-vacation-tips

Peglar, T. (2017, August 14). *Grand prismatic spring at Yellowstone's midway geyser basin*. Yellowstone National Park. https://www.yellowstonepark.com/things-to-do/geysers-hot-springs/grand-prismatic-midway-geyser-basin/

Peglar, T. (2020, July 23). *Into the deep on the Bright Angel trail*. Grand Canyon National Park Trips. https://www.mygrandcanyonpark.com/things-to-do/hiking-trails/bright-angel-trail/

Peglar, T. (2021, May 2). *4 Sides of the Grand Canyon: North, South, West plus Havasu Falls*. Grand Canyon National Park Trips. https://www.mygrandcanyonpark.com/park/places/park-access-overview/

Penn2Flow. (2017, May 18). *Exploring the Smithsonian national zoo at Washington DC!* Www.youtube.com. https://youtu.be/RYBQHl0WjRM

Pigeon Forge Department of Tourism. (2020). *Dollywood in Pigeon Forge, TN - Dollywood theme park, rides & shows*. My Pigeon Forge. https://www.mypigeonforge.com/things-to-do/dollywood

Pigeon Forge Department of Tourism. (2022a). *Arcade city at the island in Pigeon Forge - great games & prizes.* My Pigeon Forge. https://www.mypigeonforge.com/business/arcade-city-at-the-island

Pigeon Forge Department of Tourism. (2022b). *Book American cabin rentals in Pigeon Forge, tn.* My Pigeon Forge. https://www.mypigeonforge.com/business/american-cabin-rentals

Pigeon Forge Department of Tourism. (2022c). *Dollywood's dreammore resort and spa - Pigeon Forge.* My Pigeon Forge. https://www.mypigeonforge.com/business/dollywood-s-dreammore-resort-and-spa

Pigeon Forge Department of Tourism. (2022d). *Official pigeon forge, tn vacation guide - family fun in pigeon forge.* My Pigeon Forge. https://www.mypigeonforge.com/

Pigeon Forge Department of Tourism. (2022e). Visit the Titanic museum attraction in Pigeon Forge, TN. *My Pigeon Forge.* https://www.mypigeonforge.com/business/titanic

Pigeon Forge Department of Tourism. (2022f). *WonderWorks - the upside down attraction in Pigeon Forge, Tennessee.* My Pigeon Forge. https://www.mypigeonforge.com/business/wonderworks

Pigeon Forge TN Cabins. (2021, January 19). *Penguin playhouse at Ripley's Aquarium of the Smokies!* Pigeon Forge TN Cabins. https://www.pigeonforgetncabins.com/gatlinburg-penguin-playhouse/

PigeonForge.com. (n.d.-a). *Pigeon Forge lodging, cabin rentals and hotels in Pigeon Forge.* PigeonForge.com. https://www.pigeonforge.com/stay-a-while/

PigeonForge.com. (n.d.-b). *Rowdy bear mountain coaster | Pigeon Forge & Gatlinburg.* PigeonForge.com. https://www.pigeonforge.com/business/rowdy-bear-mountain-adventure-park/

Pigeonforge.com. (n.d.). *Pigeon forge, tn: Family travel destination.* PigeonForge.com. https://www.pigeonforge.com/

Pletcher, K. (n.d.). *Yellowstone lake | lake, Wyoming, United States.* Encyclopedia Britannica. https://www.britannica.com/place/Yellowstone-Lake

Rafting in the Smokies. (2022). *Pigeon River rafting | ziplining | ropes | rock climbing | Gatlinburg TN.* Rafting in the Smokies. https://raftinginthesmokies.com/

Recreation.gov. (2022). *Washington monument, national mall and memorial parks.* Recreation.gov. https://www.recreation.gov/ticket/facility/234635

Ripley Entertainment Inc. (2022). *Penguin profiles.* Ripley's Aquarium of the Smokies. https://www.ripleyaquariums.com/gatlinburg/penguin-profile/

Ripley Entertainment Inc. (2022). *Penguin playhouse.* Ripley's Aquarium of the Smokies. https://www.ripleyaquariums.com/gatlinburg/whats-inside/penguin-playhouse/

Rockin' HK Outfitters. (2022). *Horseback riding near Yellowstone | chico hot springs | rockin HK.* Rockinhk.com. https://rockinhk.com/chico-barn/?utm_source=AllTrips&utm_campaign=AllTrips-

AllYellowstonePark.com&utm_medium=referral&utm_content=/summer_recreation/horseback_riding

Rogerson, M. (2021, November 14). *Things to do at the Grand Canyon with kids*. Mum on the Move. https://www.mumonthemove.com/things-to-do-at-the-grand-canyon-with-kids/#Grand_Canyon_Tours

Rowdy Bear Mountain. (2022). *Alpine mountain coaster - rowdy bear mountain in Gatlinburg*. Rowdy Bear Mountain. https://www.rowdybearmountain.com/gatlinburg/alpine-coaster/

Scottsdale Travel Chick. (2021, June 30). *Visitors guide to Washington DC's national mall - how to do it, what to see, fun facts*. Www.youtube.com. https://youtu.be/HhfmRnJLM8c

Scrunchie Face and Friends. (2019, April 29). *Butterfly pavilion- museum of natural history!* Www.youtube.com. https://youtu.be/lD9wW2JJWJM

ShoWare. (2022). *Tickets | skypod observation deck experience*. The STRAT Ticketing. https://tickets.thestrat.com/eventperformances.asp?evt=4

Simpleview. (2022a). *Breakout games | Gatlinburg, TN 37738*. Www.gatlinburg.com. https://www.gatlinburg.com/listing/breakout-games/1275/

Simpleview. (2022b). *SMO rafting | Gatlinburg, TN 37738*. Www.gatlinburg.com. https://www.gatlinburg.com/listing/smo-rafting/750/

simpleview. (2022). *Moonshine mountain coaster | Gatlinburg, TN 37738*. Www.gatlinburg.com.

https://www.gatlinburg.com/listing/moonshine-mountain-coaster/319/

Smith, C., & Bird, J. (2020, November 30). *20 Grand Canyon quotes to encapsulate your bucket list trip*. Walk My World. https://www.walkmyworld.com/posts/grand-canyon-quotes

Smithsonian. (n.d.). *Visit | Smithsonian national museum of natural history*. Naturalhistory.si.edu. https://naturalhistory.si.edu/visit

Smithsonian. (2018). *National air and space museum*. National Air and Space Museum. https://airandspace.si.edu/

Smoky Mountain Alpine Coaster. (2021). *Smoky mountain alpine coaster*. Smoky Mountain Alpine Coaster. http://www.smokymountainalpinecoaster.com/

Smoky Mountain Outdoors. (2022a). *Booking*. Book.singenuity.com. https://book.singenuity.com/57/package/

Smoky Mountain Outdoors. (2022b). *Whitewater rafting in Tennessee - white water attraction near Gatlinburg TN - Pigeon Forge rafting*. Whitewater Rafting in Tennessee - White Water Attraction near Gatlinburg TN - Pigeon Forge Rafting. https://www.smokymountainrafting.com/

SmokyMountains.com. (2021, May 21). *40+ outdoor quotes to inspire your great smoky mountain adventure*. Smokymountains.com. https://smokymountains.com/park/blog/40-outdoor-quotes-inspire-great-smoky-mountain-adventure/

Stemple, R., & Atlas Obscura. (2017, May 16). *Carousel on the national mall*. Atlas Obscura. https://www.atlasobscura.com/places/national-mall-carousel

Sullivan, C. (2022, January 15). *Dollywood prices 2022 | complete guide to Dollywood tickets*. PigeonForge.com. https://www.pigeonforge.com/dollywood-prices/

Sweetours. (2020, November 16). *Reasons to visit Grand Canyon - Sweetours Grand Canyon tours*. Sweetours Las Vegas to Grand Canyon Tours. https://sweetours.com/top-4-reasons-to-visit-grand-canyon/

Tennessee Department of Tourism. (2022a). *Anakeesta | things to do in the smokies with kids | tn vacation*. Www.tnvacation.com. https://www.tnvacation.com/kidreviewed/anakeesta

Tennessee Department of Tourism. (2022b). *Arcadia in Gatlinburg, TN - Tennessee vacation*. Www.tnvacation.com. https://www.tnvacation.com/local/gatlinburg-arcadia

Tennessee Department of Tourist Development. (2022). *Anakeesta | Gatlinburg, tn 37738*. Www.gatlinburg.com. https://www.gatlinburg.com/listing/anakeesta/326/

The Canyon.com. (n.d.). *Havasu falls & Havasupai falls Arizona - hike, permit & trip tips*. Www.thecanyon.com. https://www.thecanyon.com/havasupai-falls

The STRAT Hotel, Casino & SkyPod. (2000). *Skyjump - the strat hotel, casino & skypod - Las Vegas, nv*. Thestrat.com. https://thestrat.com/attractions/skyjump

The STRAT Hotel, Casino & SkyPod. (2018, June 27). *SkyJump 2018 youtube*. Www.youtube.com. https://youtu.be/0sWyqzqVSeQ

The STRAT Hotel, Casino & SkyPod. (2022a). *Skyjump - the strat hotel, casino & skypod - Las Vegas, nv*. Thestrat.com. https://thestrat.com/attractions/skyjump

The STRAT Hotel, Casino & SkyPod. (2022b). *Thrill rides - the strat hotel, casino & skypod - Las Vegas, nv*. Thestrat.com. https://thestrat.com/attractions/thrill-rides

Theme Park Worldwide. (2022, January 12). *Adventuredome Circus Circus Las Vegas vlog january 2022*. Www.youtube.com. https://youtu.be/v3dBq8hj_zA

thetattooedtravelers. (2020, October 25). *A guide to the Treasure Island hotel on the Las Vegas strip*. The Tattooed Travelers. https://www.thetattooedtravelers.com/treasure-island-hotel/

thingstodoinlasvegas. (2016a, July 26). *Treasure Island (TI) hotel and casino*. Things to Do in Las Vegas. https://thingstodoinlasvegas.com/treasure-island/

thingstodoinlasvegas. (2016b, October 3). *See circus acts at Circus Circus hotel and casino*. Things to Do in Las Vegas. https://thingstodoinlasvegas.com/circus-acts/

thingstodoinlasvegas.com. (n.d.). *On strip attractions archives*. Things to Do in Las Vegas. https://thingstodoinlasvegas.com/category/attractions/on-strip-attractions/

thingstodoinlasvegas.com. (2016a, July 27). *Mystère: Family fun*. Things to Do in Las Vegas. https://thingstodoinlasvegas.com/mystere/

thingstodoinlasvegas.com. (2016b, October 3). *Experience the avengers experience at Treasure Island*. Things to Do in Las Vegas. https://thingstodoinlasvegas.com/treasure-island-avengers/

thingstodoinlasvegas.com. (2016c, November 21). *Adventuredome Las Vegas | fun for all ages at Circus Circus*. Things to Do in Las Vegas. https://thingstodoinlasvegas.com/adventuredome-las-vegas/

TicketSmarter. (2022). *Cirque du soleil - mystere tickets sun, oct 9, 2022 7:00 pm in Las Vegas, NV at mystère theatre at treasure island - Las Vegas*. Www.ticketsmarter.com. https://www.ticketsmarter.com/e/cirque-du-soleil-mystere-tickets-las-vegas-10-9-2022-mystere-theatre-at-treasure-island-las-vegas/4956450

TitanicPigeonForge. (n.d.-a). *Hours - Titanic museum attraction at Pigeon Forge, TN*. Titanic Pigeon Forge. https://titanicpigeonforge.com/tickets/titanic-pigeon-forge-hours/

TitanicPigeonForge. (n.d.-b). *Titanic Pigeon Forge | ticket selection*. Tickets.titanicattraction.com. https://tickets.titanicattraction.com/WebStore/shop/viewitems.aspx?cg=pf&c=pfga&_ga=2.98896798.1224880544.1663147163-672681285.1663147163

TitanicPigeonForge.com. (n.d.-a). *Events at Titanic museum attraction in Pigeon Forge, TN*. Titanic Pigeon Forge. https://titanicpigeonforge.com/titanic-pigeon-forge-events/#lego

TitanicPigeonForge.com. (n.d.-b). *Welcome aboard Titanic museum attraction in Pigeon Forge, TN*. Titanic Pigeon Forge. https://titanicpigeonforge.com/

Touropia. (2021, May 21). *10 best places to visit in Florida - travel video*. Www.youtube.com. https://youtu.be/MQROYY0dY9A

Travel Best Bets. (n.d.). *11 reasons to use a travel agent for your next vacation*. Travel Best Bets. https://travelbestbets.com/11-reasons-to-use-a-travel-agent-for-your-next-vacation/

Travel Safe - Abroad. (2022). *How safe is Las Vegas for travel? (2022 updated) ★ travel safe - abroad*. Travel Safe - Abroad. https://www.travelsafe-abroad.com/united-states/las-vegas/

Traveling Tipps. (2021, June 7). *How to see Washington DC's NATIONAL MALL in ONE DAY*. Www.youtube.com. https://youtu.be/4wsz5swiZPA

Treasure island hotel Las Vegas location - google search. (n.d.). Www.google.com. Retrieved 202 C.E., from https://www.google.com/search?client=safari&rls=en&q=treasure+island+hotel+las+vegas+location&ie=UTF-8&oe=UTF-8

Treasure Island Las Vegas. (n.d.). *Mystère by Cirque du Soleil | shows in Las Vegas - Treasure Island*. Treasureisland.com. https://treasureisland.com/shows/2/mystere-by-cirque-du-soleil

Treaure Island Las Vegas. (n.d.). *Marvel Avengers S.T.A.T.I.O.N. at Treasure Island Las Vegas - Treasure Island*. Treasureisland.com. https://treasureisland.com/shows/69/marvel-avengers-station

Trip Hacks DC. (2017, May 14). *7 tips for seeing the monuments and memorials in DC*. Www.youtube.com. https://youtu.be/wf-V3aLMJqg

Trip Indicator LCC. (2022). *5 top Yellowstone national park cruise & boat tours | compare price 2022*. Www.tripindicator.com.

https://www.tripindicator.com/yellowstone-national-park-top-boat-cruises-sailing-tours/1/22411/N/3

Tripadvisor. (n.d.). *Circus Circus hotel & casino Las Vegas $29 ($64) - updated 2022 prices & reviews - NV*. Tripadvisor. https://www.tripadvisor.com/Hotel_Review-g45963-d91770-Reviews-Circus_Circus_Hotel_Casino_Las_Vegas-Las_Vegas_Nevada.html

Turner, M. (2021, September 27). *Stats: 88% of families are likely to travel in next 12 months*. Travel Agent Central. https://www.travelagentcentral.com/your-business/stats-88-families-are-likely-travel-next-12-months

United States Botanic Garden. (n.d.). *Welcome to United States botanic garden | United States botanic garden*. Www.usbg.gov. https://www.usbg.gov/

USGS. (2022, August 2). Monthly update of activity at Yellowstone volcano for august 1, 2022 from mammoth hot springs. Www.youtube.com. https://youtu.be/xyl59gYMNjs

vegas.com. (2022). *Skypod observation deck experience*. Vegas.com. https://www.vegas.com/attractions/on-the-strip/stratosphere-tower/

Viator. (n.d.-a). *2-Day white water rafting tour through the Grand Canyon from Las Vegas*. Viator. https://www.viator.com/tours/Las-Vegas/2-Day-White-Water-Rafting-Tour-through-the-Grand-Canyon-from-Las-Vegas/d684-5167P5?SSAID=1404671&aid=sas0_132440_1404671&mcid=43009&rel=sponsored&SSAIDDATA=SSCID%5F81k6%5Fcnlmy

Viator. (n.d.-b). *45-minute helicopter flight over the Grand Canyon from Tusayan, Arizona*. Viator. https://www.viator.com/tours/Grand-Canyon-National-Park/45-minute-Helicopter-Flight-Over-the-Grand-Canyon-from-Tusayan-Arizona/d815-18678CS?SSAID=1404671&aid=sas0_132440_1404671&mcid=43009&rel=sponsored&SSAIDDATA=SSCID%5F81k6%5Fcnkxy

VisitArizona.com. (n.d.). *A guide to visiting Havasu falls the "right way."* Visit Arizona. https://www.visitarizona.com/like-a-local/a-guide-to-visiting-havasu-falls-the-right-way/

Vyjay, S. N. (2018, July 19). *5 reasons why a family vacation is important - family holidays.* Travel Blog/Voyager. https://imvoyager.com/reasons-why-a-family-vacation-is-important/

Wadzinski, G. (2015, October 1). *Grand Canyon junior ranger programs for kids.* Grand Canyon National Park Trips. https://www.mygrandcanyonpark.com/things-to-do/park-itineraries/junior-ranger/

Wadzinski, G. (2022a, March 17). *Here's how to see Havasu falls.* Grand Canyon National Park Trips. https://www.mygrandcanyonpark.com/things-to-do/natural-wonders/waterfalls-grand-canyon/

Wadzinski, G. (2022b, June 8). *Hike rim-to-rim in the Grand Canyon.* Grand Canyon National Park Trips. https://www.mygrandcanyonpark.com/things-to-do/hiking-trails/hike-rim-to-rim-grand-canyon/?itm_source=parsely-api

Wadzinski, G., & Peglar, T. (2022, March 16). *How to raft the Grand Canyon.* Grand Canyon National Park Trips.

https://www.mygrandcanyonpark.com/things-to-do/rafting/grand-canyon-rafting-essentials/?itm_source=parsely-api

Washington.org. (2016, April 18). *The Smithsonian castle: Gateway to museums & history*. Washington.org. https://washington.org/dc-guide-to/smithsonian-institution-building-castle

Washington.org. (2019, January 11). *Visiting the Smithsonian national air and space museum in Washington, DC*. Washington.org. https://washington.org/dc-guide-to/smithsonian-national-air-and-space-museum

Washington.org. (2022a). *How can I tour the monuments & memorials in Washington, DC? | Washington DC*. Washington.org. https://washington.org/visit-dc/tours-of-washington-dc-monuments-memorials

Washington.org. (2022b). *United States Botanic Garden | Washington DC*. Washington.org. https://washington.org/find-dc-listings/united-states-botanic-garden

WDD. (2022a). *Gatlinburg craftsmen's fair - Gatlinburg attractions | things to do in Gatlinburg, TN*. Gatlinburg Attractions. https://www.gatlinburg-attractions.com/attraction/gatlinburg-craftsmens-fair/

WDD. (2022b). *Ripley's penguin playhouse - Gatlinburg attractions | things to do in Gatlinburg, TN*. Gatlinburg Attractions. https://www.gatlinburg-attractions.com/attraction/ripleys-penguin-playhouse/

WikiMedia. (2022, May 31). *Hayden valley*. Wikipedia. https://en.wikipedia.org/wiki/Hayden_Valley

Wikipedia. (2022a, September 14). *Tidal basin*. Wikipedia. https://en.wikipedia.org/wiki/Tidal_Basin

Wikipedia. (2022b, September 16). *Grand prismatic spring*. Wikipedia. https://en.m.wikipedia.org/wiki/Grand_Prismatic_Spring

Wikipedia Contributors. (2018, November 15). *Lincoln memorial*. Wikipedia; Wikimedia Foundation. https://en.wikipedia.org/wiki/Lincoln_Memorial

Wikipedia Contributors. (2019a, February 17). *I Have a Dream*. Wikipedia; Wikimedia Foundation. https://en.wikipedia.org/wiki/I_Have_a_Dream

Wikipedia Contributors. (2019b, April 11). *National Zoological Park (United States)*. Wikipedia; Wikimedia Foundation. https://en.wikipedia.org/wiki/National_Zoological_Park_(United_States)

Wikipedia Contributors. (2019c, May 31). *National museum of natural history*. Wikipedia; Wikimedia Foundation. https://en.wikipedia.org/wiki/National_Museum_of_Natural_History

Wikipedia Contributors. (2019d, November 3). *National mall*. Wikipedia; Wikimedia Foundation. https://en.wikipedia.org/wiki/National_Mall

wikivoyage. (n.d.). *Gatlinburg – travel guide at wikivoyage*. En.wikivoyage.org. https://en.wikivoyage.org/wiki/Gatlinburg

Witze, A. (2019). A deeper understanding of the Grand Canyon. *Knowable Magazine*. https://doi.org/10.1146/knowable-022619-1

WonderWorks. (2021). *Pigeon Forge attractions | things to do in Pigeon Forge*. WonderWorks Pigeon Forge. https://www.wonderworksonline.com/pigeon-forge/

Yellowstone Mountain Guides. (2015, May 5). *Horseback trailrides*. Yellowstone Mountain Guides. https://yellowstone-guides.com/horseback-trailrides/?utm_source=AllTrips&utm_campaign=AllTrips-AllYellowstonePark.com&utm_medium=referral&utm_content=/summer_recreation/horseback_riding

Yellowstone National Park Lodges. (2017a, April 26). *Geyser gazers*. Yellowstone National Park Lodges. https://www.yellowstonenationalparklodges.com/adventure/land-adventures/geyser-gazers/

Yellowstone National Park Lodges. (2017b, April 27). *Yellowstone lake butte sunset tour | Yellowstone national park lodge*. Yellowstone National Park Lodges. https://www.yellowstonenationalparklodges.com/adventure/land-adventures/yellowstone-lake-butte-sunset-tour/

Yellowstone National Park Lodges. (2019). *Transportation to Yellowstone | Yellowstone national park lodges*. Yellowstone National Park Lodges. https://www.yellowstonenationalparklodges.com/stay/plan/transportation/

Yellowstone National Park Lodges. (2022a). *Adventures in Yellowstone national park*. Yellowstone National Park Lodges. https://www.yellowstonenationalparklodges.com/adventures/

Yellowstone National Park Lodges. (2022b). *Custom guided ski tour-mammoth*. Yellowstone National Park Lodges.

https://www.yellowstonenationalparklodges.com/adventure/winter-activities-at-mammoth/custom-guided-ski-tour/

Yellowstone National Park Lodges. (2022c). *Grand canyon day tour mammoth*. Yellowstone National Park Lodges. https://www.yellowstonenationalparklodges.com/adventure/winter-activities-at-mammoth/grand-canyon-day-tour-mammoth/

Yellowstone National Park Lodges. (2022d). *Norris geyser basin tour*. Yellowstone National Park Lodges. https://www.yellowstonenationalparklodges.com/adventure/winter-activities-at-mammoth/norris-geyser-basin-tour/

Yellowstone National Park Lodges. (2022e). *Water adventures | Yellowstone national park lodge*. Yellowstone National Park Lodges. https://www.yellowstonenationalparklodges.com/adventures/water-adventures/

Yellowstone National Park Lodges. (2022f). *winter adventures*. Yellowstone National Park Lodges. https://www.yellowstonenationalparklodges.com/adventures/winter-adventures/

Yellowstone National Park Trips. (2020, July 21). *Swim in Yellowstone's boiling river*. Yellowstone National Park. https://www.yellowstonepark.com/things-to-do/rafting-water-activities/swim-yellowstones-boiling-river/

Made in the USA
Las Vegas, NV
15 April 2024

88725456R00095